I am delighted to see this text! It will be very, very helpful right across ᴛʜᴇ Majorᵢₜᵧ and also useful for many supervisors in the West. I kept thinking back to my own time as a PhD student in Cambridge and how different things were then! . . . The integration of the evangelical, spiritual, pastoral, and ethical dimensions in with the academic, practical and technical ones, works very well. This is a good "Christian" read, as well as a good "academic" handbook.

Christopher J. H. Wright
International Ministry Director, Langham Partnership

I consider this handbook to be quite outstanding. I have not read anything of this kind before, designed as it is for doctoral supervisors within the evangelical community. I greatly appreciate the emphasis Ian Shaw places on spiritual formation and pastoral care. He faces up to evangelical challenges and offers solid and creative suggestions. The case studies and the questions are excellent. I commend this enthusiastically.

Ian Randall
Senior Research Fellow,
International Baptist Theological Study Centre, Amsterdam

This book is brilliant! I wish I had had something like this twenty years ago! If partner institutions can implement a good proportion of all the recommended good practice, I suspect that they will be doing better than many much better-known programmes around the world. I particularly enjoyed reading the material on surface learning and deep learning, and the whole issue of critical thinking. Here and in so many places through the book, there is really practical guidance about *how* to help develop such skills. Often, I think, supervisors recognise such weaknesses in students, but if these issues haven't really been a problem for them personally they find it hard to know how to help students develop such skills. I hope and pray this book will be warmly welcomed and widely used.

Stephen Travis
former Vice-Principal of St John's College, Nottingham

Everything you need to know about doctoral supervision is in this handbook! It is both scholarly and practical, with emphasis on the holistic formation of evangelical scholars. This comprehensive guide is a valuable gift to global theological education. It will be a useful resource in equipping our doctoral supervisors and enhancing the quality of doctoral programs in theological institutions in the Majority World.

Theresa Roco Lua
Secretary of Accreditation and Educational Development,
Asia Theological Association
Dean, Asia Graduate School of Theology, Philippines

ICETE Series

Handbook for Supervisors of Doctoral Students in Evangelical Theological Institutions

ICETE International Council for Evangelical Theological Education
strengthening evangelical theological education through international cooperation

Langham
GLOBAL LIBRARY

Handbook for Supervisors of Doctoral Students in Evangelical Theological Institutions

Ian J. Shaw

with

Kevin E. Lawson

Series Editor

Riad Kassis

ICETE International Council for Evangelical Theological Education
strengthening evangelical theological education through international cooperation

Langham
GLOBAL LIBRARY

© 2015 by Ian J. Shaw

Published 2015 by Langham Global Library
an imprint of Langham Publishing
www.langhampublishing.org

Langham Publishing and its imprints are a ministry of Langham Partnership

Langham Partnership
PO Box 296, Carlisle, Cumbria CA3 9WZ, UK
www.langham.org

ISBNs:
978-1-78368-096-2 Print
978-1-78368-098-6 Mobi
978-1-78368-097-9 ePub
978-1-78368-099-3 PDF

British Library Cataloguing in Publication Data
A catalogue record for this book is available from the British Library

ISBN: 978-1-78368-096-2

Cover & Book Design: projectluz.com

This book is dedicated to the more than 400 Langham Scholars who have fulfilled the vision of John Stott by receiving training to doctoral level in theological studies in order to serve in the Majority World in the vital task of training pastors, teachers and Christian leaders in strategic leadership positions.

Contents

Preface

This handbook grows out of many years of experience working as a doctoral supervisor and doctoral thesis examiner, and running a doctoral program in a major UK theological college. Since moving from lecturing in a seminary seven years ago my work has involved leading Langham Partnership's scholarship ministry, which each year is providing scholarships for up to ninety doctoral scholars from the Majority World, around half of whom study in institutions in the Majority World, and the rest in the West. All are studying in the theological disciplines. In supporting Langham Scholars I have seen them receive supervision that rates from excellent, to good, to average and sadly, sometimes, very poor, in a range of contexts across the globe. This book is designed to promote approaches to supervision that ensure that the experience of all is excellent.

As part of this widespread desire for excellence, in 2010 I was invited to be part of the International Council for Evangelical Theological Education (ICETE) Doctoral Initiative, which began with a remarkable meeting in Beirut of leaders of global theological education at doctoral level, out of which the landmark Beirut Benchmarks emerged. To explain and apply the Beirut Benchmarks I was asked to write a series of *Best Practice Guidelines for Doctoral Programs*, which Langham Global Library has also published for ICETE. These documents are regularly referenced in this work, and set out the key attainment levels in provision and delivery all programs should aim for.

Over the past years I have also been invited to give seminars around the world on the topic of doctoral supervision, and out of those seminars this book has been developed. I have learned greatly from the participants in the different contexts in which they have been delivered. Each group of seminar participants have reflected that although there are a number of generic texts about doctoral supervision in the secular context, there is little that deals with supervision from the perspective of the supervisor who is an evangelical Christian, and who teaches in an evangelical theological institution. While many of the issues faced in supporting doctoral students are the same as those in secular universities, there are some significant differences in ethos and approach (although not in academic level). This handbook seeks to give particular attention to these.

I am very grateful for assistance of Dr Kevin Lawson with some parts of this handbook. He has contributed material to a number of sections of the text from his wide experience in the USA of leading doctoral programs, supervising doctoral students, chairing doctoral committees, and serving as an examiner of others.

My prayer is that this handbook will serve evangelical Christians engaged in this important task, by providing a tool that is practical, and relevant, and which invites self-reflection towards best practice. It can therefore be used on an individual basis, but it also lends itself to group study with colleagues. The case studies in the chapters that follow are based on real examples I have come across, but all names and personal details have been changed. They are included to open up the realities and complexities of doctoral supervision, and to help think through strategies to deal with the type of issues that can arise. I hope that this handbook will deepen the understanding of the task and the sense of fulfilment and satisfaction in this supervisory role. The primary intended audience for this handbook is those involved in doctoral supervision in seminaries, theological colleges and Christian universities which are evangelical, but the principles set out here will also be of help to evangelical supervisors who work in a secular environment and whose colleagues on a supervisory team might not be evangelicals, or make any Christian profession at all. The ethos and approaches suggested in this handbook can also readily be applied in these contexts with appropriate adjustments.

The handbook seeks to promote the integration in their studies that evangelical students long for – of excellent training in academic skills and also a strong focus on the spiritual and pastoral dynamics of supervision. Theological education is a key aspect of Christian mission. Training doctoral students is therefore an important part of the mission of God, for most will go on to play strategic roles in training pastors, teachers and other Christian leaders. I want to see global evangelical theological education strengthened, deepened, and extended, so that it is better able to train the next generation of godly leaders for the church. I pray that God will use this book as a contribution to this vital task, and for his greater glory.

Dr Ian J. Shaw, PhD
Associate International Director, Langham Partnership Scholars Ministry
Co-Chair ICETE Doctoral Initiative Steering Committee
Honorary Fellow, Faculty of Theology, University of Edinburgh, Scotland

with

Dr Kevin E. Lawson, EdD
Director, PhD and EdD programs in Educational Studies
Professor of Christian Education; Talbot School of Theology, Biola University,
La Mirada, California

1

The Work and Qualifications of the Evangelical Doctoral Supervisor

Supervising doctoral students has been one of the most satisfying and enjoyable aspects of my Christian ministry in the academic context. It has been a very demanding task. It has its great joys, and sometimes deep frustrations. Yet, seeing students emerge as equipped, qualified, and engaged thinkers, teachers and researchers, who have taken on board your guidance and instruction, modeling what you have sought to teach, and now making a contribution to your discipline, is one of the best investments of your time and energies.

But how do you do it well?

You might have just been approached by a senior academic leader and invited to supervise a doctoral student, and you are wondering am I ready for this, or 'what have I got myself into'? You may even have been asked to read this handbook as you prepare for the role.

Maybe you have been supervising doctoral students for some time, and have picked up this handbook to enable you to reflect afresh on your practice. Perhaps you are thinking – does this remain a good use of my time?

What follows is based on a wide range of experience – from the past fifteen years spent as a supervisor and examiner of doctoral students; from running a doctoral program in an evangelical seminary; and through offering support, advice and training over the past seven years to more than 150 doctoral students while helping to lead the Langham Partnership Scholarship program, which supports Christian leaders from the Majority World. They study at major institutions running well-established doctoral programs in Europe and North America, and also newer programs in the Majority World. Across those institutions, in both the Majority World and the West, I have seen students experience a range of supervisory styles and approaches, which rank from the very good, to sadly, sometimes, the very bad. It is hoped that the suggestions offered here will help towards extending best practice, and this handbook should be read in conjunction with ICETE's *Best Practice Guidelines*.[1] It is a role every supervisor, no matter how experienced, needs to go on learning about and growing in.

A Word about Terminology

The research doctorate is a global product, but even the names given to the qualification vary from context to context. The primary focus of this handbook is the research-based doctoral qualification, usually known as Doctor of Philosophy (PhD or DPhil), and which is similar to the Doctor of Theology (DTh). Those supervising the work of Professional Doctorates in theology may derive significant benefit from this book (Doctor of Missiology, Doctor of Education), although the skills tested in the professional doctorate, and the way this testing takes place, are somewhat different to the PhD – these differences are set out in the ICETE Beirut Benchmarks for Research Doctorates, and the Beirut Benchmarks Adaptation for Professional Doctorates.[2] Those supervising dissertations written at masters level may also find valuable material here.

The term 'doctoral supervisor' is used in this handbook to refer to the person, or members of a team, who work closely in offering direction and advice in the major research project that lies at the heart of the doctorate. Some programs use the terms 'thesis advisor', 'thesis director', 'thesis mentor', 'thesis promoter', 'director of studies', and 'chair of dissertation committee' for this role, but for the sake of clarity, the single term 'supervisor' will be used throughout this handbook.

Even the term 'doctoral thesis' is subject to variation, and in some academic cultures 'doctoral dissertation' is preferred, or 'research project'. Again, for clarity, 'thesis' is the term adopted here. We are talking about an original major research project of 75,000 to 100,000 words, taking anything between two and five years full-time to write.

Are you the right person for the job?

This is an important question to ask, and keep on asking. It is possible that a person once qualified to supervise at doctoral level is no longer suitable. The supervisor's role is pivotal in the success of the doctoral student.

Doctoral supervision is a big responsibility. If a student fails a course in a program at another level, it may be the student's fault, or that of a whole series of teachers in other classes in addition to your own role. At doctoral level you stand much more exposed. The primary responsibility still lies with the student, but then with the supervisor.

---

1. I. Shaw, *Best Practice Guidelines for Doctoral Programs* (Carlisle: Langham Global Library, 2015).
2. These are found in Shaw, *Best Practice*.

Such a responsibility may make you feel a little nervous – as indeed it should. Supervising doctoral students is not to be taken lightly, or done half-heartedly, and certainly not done by those who are unqualified.

Are you sure you are qualified and equipped to bear this responsibility?

Supervision is primarily an academic role, but it also contains certain aspects that have a pastoral and leadership training dimension, although these should not interfere with the primary academic responsibilities.

The ICETE *Best Practice Guidelines*[3] set out the qualifications for doctoral supervisors working in evangelical theological institutions. As well as having excellent qualifications, those who are supervisors need to be established teachers and mature Christian leaders. They need to be able to model godly Christian scholarship, and be committed to both the academic and spiritual formation of those they supervise.

This means that:

- Doctoral supervisors should be in good standing in both the academic community and in the local Christian church.
- They should be capable of providing both academic support and demonstrating appropriate pastoral sensitivity to the needs of the student.
- They should have demonstrated the ability to integrate academic and spiritual excellence.
- Where the institution requires this, supervisors need to be willing to sign its statement of faith or confessional basis.
- Doctoral supervisors need to be appropriately qualified and have the experience, skills, and subject knowledge to support, train, and monitor the research students assigned to them.

The primary supervisor of a doctoral thesis / dissertation needs to be qualified with an earned research doctorate (PhD, DTh). This should be in the field in which the doctoral student intends to research. Some educational systems (e.g. in Eastern Europe) also require a further post-doctoral qualification, such as the Doctor of Habilitation degree, before it is possible to supervise doctoral students. In some cases, someone with a doctorate such as EdD or DMiss degree will be a suitable supervisor if their degree involved a significant amount of original empirical research, research methods training courses, and writing a substantial research thesis. The primary supervisor of a doctoral thesis should already have gained experience as a supervisor of independent research (usually at masters level), and have been teaching for several years. It is normal to gain further experience

---

3. Shaw, *Best Practice*, Section 16.

by initially working as a joint supervisor, or second supervisor, of a doctoral student, in order to build the skills needed, before becoming a primary supervisor.

A supervisor needs to have expertise and academic currency in areas that closely match the intended research of the doctoral student. Evidence for this will be measured in terms of recent publications and research activity. Academic faculty who have not continued to write or research since the completion of their doctorate should not be active as supervisors – students need to be supported by those who are scholarly-current, and research-active. It should be remembered that ongoing research activity feeds into both good academic supervision and good teaching, so research supervisors need to maintain research-level academic currency as part of their faculty development activity. Supervisors or mentors of doctoral candidates also need to have regular opportunities for faculty development and training related to the performance of the role, as will be noted later.

A Biblical and Theological Rationale for Supervision

The evangelical academic who is asked to work as a supervisor of doctoral research should develop a biblical and theological rationale for their work. They also need to be able to help the evangelical doctoral student to do the same for the task they are undertaking, and they will need help in order to develop this.

This should be centered on the recognition that knowledge is not just an academic matter. This was recognized in the motto of the University of Aberdeen, founded as long ago as 1495 by William Elphinstone, Bishop of Aberdeen, *'Initium sapientiae timor Dei'*, (the beginning of wisdom is fear of the Lord).

Helping a student who is an evangelical Christian to gain a PhD is more than just assisting them to gain large amounts of information, although that is important. It is also more than helping them to develop well-honed critical thinking skills, although that is vital. Wisdom, in the biblical sense, draws together reason, action and faith. In the evangelical context, doctoral study is a spiritual exercise, just as much as an intellectual exercise. This is well expressed in the *ICETE Beirut Benchmarks*, – *'it involves right belief and committed trust in the living God ("the fear of the LORD is the first principle of wisdom.")'*[4] Taking on a role in the supervision of a doctoral student engages with significant issues of faith, both the personal faith of the student and the supervisor, and also that of the wider faith community.

This will mean that doctoral studies undertaken in an evangelical seminary or university must have the same academic rigor and standards as those undertaken in a secular university, but evangelical student and supervisor will be approaching the

---

4. Shaw, *Best Practice*, Section 1.

process from different foundational principles. The experience of doctoral education in a theological seminary or Christian university will be notably different to that undertaken in another secular institution. Based on a fully rounded biblical understanding of knowledge and wisdom, the evangelical student should benefit from working in a rich and fulfilling context in which excellence in both academic and spiritual disciplines is consciously nurtured. Part of the role of the doctoral supervisor is to develop that context.

One response to the eighteenth-century Enlightenment was an attempt to place Christianity above the rationalist critique by drawing a distinction between matters of faith and religious feeling, and those of the mind. This serious dichotomy still needs to be addressed and overcome, especially at doctoral level. The evangelical doctoral supervisor is working to enable evangelical doctoral students to creatively and humbly use the rationality God has graciously given to humans made in his own image. Jesus invited his disciples to worship God with heart, and soul, and mind. This means that academic research is an aspect of loving God with the mind (Matt 22:37–40): biblically, the discontinuity between the mind and personal spirituality does not exist. Thinking profound thoughts, and encouraging our students to think equally profound thoughts, is one dimension of our love to God with heart, soul, and mind.

The Holistic Dimension

Doctoral study needs to be understood holistically. It impinges on the whole life and character of both evangelical supervisor and student. There must be continuity between their Christian character and their research work. Student and supervisor need to demonstrate both integrity and integration in all aspects of their work. Spiritual excellence must stand alongside academic rigor and the highest possible standards of research and reflection. The supervisor's own academic skills and research excellence need to be accompanied by appropriate living in the world to reflect God's calling and participation in God's mission, and thereby to model this for students. Even where evangelical students and evangelical supervisors are working within the constraints of the secular university, which need to be carefully respected, they should still be motivated by the same principles of Christian integrity and integration, even if the context is not designed explicitly to facilitate that.

Excellence in Supervision

Whatever the evangelical believer puts her or his hand to should be done with a desire for excellence, and to glorify God. As Paul urges his readers in 2 Corinthians 8:7 to 'excel in everything', including 'in faith, in speech, in knowledge, in complete earnestness and in your love for us,' so the doctoral supervisor should aspire to excel in their supervisory work, and the research and teaching that underpins it. There needs to be an absolute commitment to safeguard academic standards, ensuring the highest national and international levels of credibility. Just because the person being supervised is a sister or brother in Christ does not mean that these standards should be lessened. But alongside this the overall desire for the student being supervised is that they not only develop a well-trained mind, but are enhanced in their abilities as Christian leaders, are spiritually formed through the process and equipped for God-honoring service.

Because the research doctorate is the highest level of academic attainment possible, the supervisor is the primary interface in supporting the student in an educational process the end product of which must, in the opinion of its examiners, match up to internationally accepted standards of doctoral education. While there will be variety in the way doctoral programs are delivered, the final product still needs to look like a doctorate, be examined to the level of a doctorate elsewhere in the world, and be recognized as such in the eyes of the global academic community, as well as by local accreditors or validators, churches, and students undertaking the program. Alongside this, the supervisor in the evangelical theological institution must ensure the doctorate is in fact the pinnacle of Christian training. It should be seen as the place where we seek to be most excellent in preparing Christian leaders for service. The successful doctoral candidate needs to be presented before the judgment of the wider Christian community as someone highly enabled and thoroughly equipped for Christian leadership, especially in an academic context.

Therefore, doctoral students and their supervisors need to undertake their work with the right ultimate motivations. As Andrew Walls has recently written:

> It is necessary to begin by distinguishing between promoting scholarship and producing PhDs. In every continent there are already enough holders of doctorates who have never contributed a jot or tittle to scholarship. There is no point in setting up factories in Africa and Asia, however efficient, to train people to jump through doctoral hoops who have no calling for scholarship and no passion (for nothing less will do) for its exercise. The pursuit of the scholarly life is a Christian vocation within God's mission to the world; in comparison with this, the quest for doctorates is frivolity.[5]

Supervisor or Dissertation Committee Appointment

Each school must develop policies and procedures for the selection and approval of the supervisor, the dissertation committee chair and other committee members.

Supervisor Model: In doctoral programs which follow the European / British model, the PhD student works with a primary supervisor and a secondary supervisor, and

---

5. A. Walls, 'World Christianity, Theological Education and Scholarship,' *Transformation* 28, no. 4 (October 2011): 235–240.

sometimes a small team of other supervisors. The supervisor may have been approached formally or informally by the student before starting the program to discuss potential research ideas, or the supervisor may be appointed directly by the institution, but all supervisory arrangements should be agreed and confirmed in writing by the institution. The roles and responsibilities of first and second supervisors should be agreed and set out in writing. It is important to ensure good and frequent communication between members of a supervisory team, and to arrange for regular meetings between them and the student. These should take place at key moments in the student's progression, including the initial stages of the research program, at progression reviews, and in assessing whether the thesis is ready for submission before an examination is arranged.

Dissertation Committee Model: In doctoral programs that follow the model common in the United States of America, each doctoral student works with a dissertation committee that both guides and evaluates their research. The resulting thesis / dissertation is similar to that in the European model, but the process of its development and defense tends to follow a different path. Once students have completed their coursework and passed their 'candidacy exam,' they move on to the thesis / dissertation phase of their program. During the coursework phase students will have taken classes that provide a foundation for their chosen area of study and helped them develop the research skills they will be using in developing and writing their thesis / dissertation. Once the coursework and candidacy exam are completed, students request the appointment of a dissertation committee to guide them through the dissertation process.

Dissertation committees can vary in size and composition. One common model would have three people serving on it: the Chair, a Second Reader, and a Third Reader. The Chair of the dissertation committee functions as the primary advisor to the student, guiding them in developing initial drafts of the various sections of the dissertation. The chair is the principal supervisor for the student, meeting often to discuss the focus and development of the dissertation, providing feedback on their writing, and helping the student set and maintain appropriate goals and boundaries for the research effort. The chair largely fulfils the principal functions of the supervisor set out throughout the rest of this book.

The second and third readers also provide guidance and feedback, but their work typically follows after the initial work done by the chair with the student, and may focus on particular aspects of the research project. These 'readers' may have expertise in an aspect of the study content, or methodology, and may be asked to take a leadership role in some aspects of the study. In other cases, they may have general background in the area of study being pursued, and serve as another 'set of eyes,' giving feedback on the argument and evidence of the study after the chair has done the initial work with the student. In some ways, the inclusion of second and third readers on the dissertation committee is similar to having a second supervisor and an external reviewer to help in evaluating the dissertation research the student carries out. Ultimately, all three must agree that the dissertation is worthy of passing and the student allowed to graduate with the doctoral degree.

While every effort should be made to secure the Chair of the dissertation committee that the student wants to work with, this must be balanced with concerns for faculty workload, striving not to overburden faculty members. It may be that if a faculty member is already carrying a heavy load of dissertation work, he or she could serve as a second supervisor, or second or third reader on the dissertation committee, instead of being the chair. In this way, the student is able to have this faculty member's perspective and assistance in the research process without his or her needing to take on the primary supervision role.

The composition of the rest of the supervisory team or the dissertation committee is often negotiated between the chair and the student. The chair may know of faculty members with particular areas of expertise who should be invited to serve on the committee. On the other hand, the student may have undertaken coursework with a faculty member who he/she feels would make a strong contribution to the committee. In some cases a scholar outside the institution may be invited to serve on the committee. You will want to think this through at a policy level within your institution so that both faculty members and students are aware of the committee recruitment and approval process and their part in it. It may not be possible for the student to have all of the people they might wish to have on their committee, but there should be a good rapport between the student and committee members. The chair should take the initiative of doing the actual recruiting of the other committee members and orienting them to the basics of the proposed study and what is being requested of them as members of the dissertation committee.

Where possible, it can be beneficial to have an initial meeting of the student with all of the members of the dissertation committee. This can be held after the student and chair have worked through an initial proposed focus and parameters of the planned study. At the meeting, the student can give a presentation of the proposed focus, scope, and rationale for the study. The committee members can then be invited to offer their thoughts, observations, questions, and ideas for the student to consider in consultation with the chair. In addition, the committee members can discuss their roles in the dissertation process and any restrictions in their schedules for consultation work. In this way, all committee members have an opportunity to speak into the initial focus and development of the study, ensuring a common understanding of what the student will be striving to accomplish and their role in the process. It can also minimize the possibility of a conflict of perspectives later, avoiding wasted work and the stress of differing expectations and feedback to the student. Where a physical meeting of all members is not possible, using Skype or another video conferencing facility can facilitate this conversation.

Working in Community

Lest this challenge and responsibility of developing spiritual and academic excellence appear too onerous a task, it should be remembered that the doctoral supervisor should be working towards this end as part of a supportive learning community. I used to tell my colleagues that the community needed to successfully train a doctoral student involves the receptionist, the janitor, the academic secretaries, computer support technicians and the librarians, other faculty, as well as the supervisor. All must wholeheartedly give themselves to the task of nurturing key skills in future leaders. This needs to be a 'learning' community, not just a community where learning takes place.

Summary

The evangelical doctoral supervisor should constantly aspire to be more Christ-like in all that they do, and say, and think; more biblical in their guiding principles; and ever more desirous of higher standards and getting the very best from their students. Supervisors need to constantly be prepared to evaluate practice, face up to mistakes, and learn from them. This handbook is designed to be a contribution to that process.

Reflective Questions

Take a few moments to reflect on:

Your own thoughts about doctoral supervision

> Are they positive or negative?

> What experiences lie behind those thoughts?

What areas are you conscious you need to work on in the area of supervision?

If you have already supervised, what was your most satisfying experience as a doctoral supervisor so far?

If you are new to supervision, what is your greatest hope for your work as a supervisor?

How will you measure success in supervision?

Further Reading

Delamont, S., P. Atkinson, and O. Parry. *Supervising the PhD: A Guide to Success.* Bristol, PA: The Society for Research into Higher Education & Open University Press, 1997.

Eley A., and R. Murray. *How to Be an Effective Supervisor.* Maidenhead: Open University Press, 2009.

Nerad, M., and M. Heggelund, eds. *Toward a Global PhD? Forces and Forms in Doctoral Education Worldwide.* Seattle: University of Washington Press, 2008.

Phillips, E. M., and D. S. Pugh. *How to Get a PhD: A Handbook for Students and their Supervisors.* Maidenhead: Open University Press, 2010. (Kindle edition available also)

Powell, S., and H. Green, eds. *The Doctorate Worldwide.* Maidenhead: Open University Press, 2007.

Shaw, I. *Best Practice Guidelines for Doctoral Programs.* Carlisle: Langham Global Library, 2015.

Taylor, Stan, and Nigel Beasley. *A Handbook for Doctoral Supervisors.* New York: Routledge, 2005.

Walker, G. E., C. M. Golde, L. Jones, A. C. Bueschel, and P. Hutchings. *The Formation of Scholars: Rethinking Doctoral Education for the Twenty-First Century.* San Francisco: Jossey-Bass, 2008. A provocative study from the USA, some of which you will agree with, some of which you won't!

Walker, M., and P. Thomson, eds. *The Routledge Doctoral Supervisor's Companion: Supporting Effective Research in Education and the Social Sciences.* New York: Routledge, 2010.

Wisker, Gina. *The Good Supervisor: Supervising Postgraduate and Undergraduate Research for Doctoral Theses and Dissertations.* New York: Palgrave MacMillan, 2005.

Higher Education Research Journals

(These journals regularly feature articles on the 'state of the art' thinking on postgraduate education and doctoral thinking.)

For example

Studies in Higher Education

Higher Education Research and Development

Journal of Further and Higher Education

2

Helping Students to Understand the Nature of the Research Task

Undertaking research is exciting, and challenging. It draws on creative and imaginative capacities, as well as demanding disciplined study, rigorous thought, and large amounts of writing.

Supervisors need to help their students understand exactly what they are expected to do when undertaking research, offer guidance about how to achieve this, and help them develop the skills they need.

What is Research?

'Research' is original investigation undertaken in order to gain knowledge and understanding. A researcher is therefore going to generate new ideas, and develop projects that lead to new or improved insights. Students will be maintaining and adding to the intellectual infrastructure of their subject or discipline.

To undertake research at the doctoral level students need to lay a foundation of knowledge, especially as it relates to research that has already been undertaken in their field. The prior study that others have undertaken needs to be analyzed, synthesized, and the implications of that for current and future research understood.

Research is a journey of discovery, which will lead to finding out new things, and devising new arguments. Students will look at documents and sources that have not previously been read and investigated, or look at them in new ways not attempted before, or by using new approaches and techniques. The supervisor has the privilege of sharing with the student on that journey, which brings its own vicarious pleasure. The supervisor derives professional and academic satisfaction from seeing their own field being advanced by the research work their students are doing. However, this needs to be done with integrity – the student's intellectual property must be respected and celebrated.

There should be a strong motivation by students, not just to know more, but also to creatively solve problems, or see particular issues more clearly. Old material can be viewed in a fresh way.

Another exciting dimension of research is not just finding out new things, but also making connections, and building bridges to other areas of knowledge. Students need help and direction in doing this.

One of the major areas supervisors interact with students about is in their written work. They regularly receive, comment on, and discuss samples of text. This process is not just assisting students in recording their findings, but also building the communication skills that students need to use in disseminating their research findings. This is vital not only for the doctorate itself, but also for future research and writing ministry. Students need to learn how to apply their research findings to current academic debates. They also need to think through how their research can serve the needs of the wider Christian community.

There may be aspects of a student's research that will relate directly to future teaching. The skills of developing research questions, undertaking analysis and synthesis, communicating findings effectively and clearly, which are vital to the research task also have significant transferable value in the writing of books, or in preparing and delivering courses of lectures.

An important outflow of research should be stimulating, creative, and effective approaches to teaching and learning, which is another way by which research findings are disseminated.

Research and the Evangelical

In some students, the supervisor will find that excitement at the potentiality of research is tempered by a very real fear. In 1941 Dr Martyn Lloyd-Jones set out what he saw as the causes of the weakness in Biblical Studies and Biblical Theology among evangelicals in the twentieth century. These included a greater emphasis on subjectivity and personal experience than upon detailed Scripture study and exposition; a heightened stress on the imminent Second Advent of Christ in the light of which thorough and in-depth scholarship was superfluous; and an emphasis on the urgency of preaching the gospel which made the slow and detailed work of scholars seem of secondary importance. Also the higher-life holiness movement stressed the cultivation of personal piety before that of the scholarly mind. Lloyd-Jones believed all these factors had led to a drastic decline in evangelical scholarship in the early decades of the twentieth century.[1]

---

1. T. A. Noble, *Research for the Academy and the Church: Tyndale House and Fellowship: The First Sixty Years* (Leicester: IVP, 2006), 34–35.

In some circles of evangelicalism, such ideas persist. Although by the time students enter doctoral studies, it is to be hoped that they do not entertain them personally, Christian friends, family, even church leaders may still do so. The supervisor may need to work these issues through with the student to help them justify their investment of time and money in research work. In response to these issues, Lloyd-Jones encouraged the foundation of Tyndale House, Cambridge, as a center for biblical research. He saw linguistic and historical scholarship as being essential in ensuring the validity and accuracy of the primary text sources for both the Bible and theology, and enabling precise understanding of biblical text to be applied in exegesis and translation. He also strongly emphasized the need for technical linguistic and textual studies to be combined with the skills of biblical theology, to enable the understanding of the theological implications of discoveries and their application.[2]

At the heart of the research thesis is 'originality' and 'newness'. In some circles of evangelicalism such concepts are still associated with biblical or confessional unorthodoxy. To discover something 'new' about Scripture or traditional theology is associated, they think, with a tendency to heresy. Students need to be helped to develop a personal 'apologetic' to counter such fears. Evangelicals can confidently undertake research on a confessional basis,[3] which acts for them as a secure foundation for their research, but this does not need to place a limit on research. While in some areas new paradigms and approaches are needed, in others there is a need to revisit and re-establish former ones based on a conviction of biblical authority, a distinctly Christian worldview, and confessional orthodoxy. Dr W. J. Martin, Lecturer in Hebrew at Liverpool University, stressed the need for informed, believing, high-level academic biblical scholarship:

> Our faith is inseparably linked with certain historical events recorded in an extensive corpus of written documents, hence its credentials are open to objective investigation. The need for a scholarly defence of the faith is as great today as ever. The qualifications required to participate in this defence can be obtained only by years of study and application.[4]

To Martin, the years of 'study and application' required for research in Old Testament studies included experience of study in Germany, a year in Rome at the Pontifical Biblical Institute, and a year studying Arabic culture in Egypt. Of course, not all researchers can afford to undertake such a range of opportunities, but his recommendation outlines the seriousness of the task. Evangelical researchers need the courage both to be trailblazers of

---

2. Noble, *Research for the Academy*, 39.

3. This is 'confession' with a small c, and is not limited to one particular Confession.

4. W. J. Martin, 'A Later Statement of the Aims of Tyndale House, 1941,' in *Research for the Academy and the Church: Tyndale House and Fellowship: The First Sixty Years*, ed. T. A. Noble (Leicester: IVP, 2006), 37.

new thinking, and also renovators and restorers of core kingdom values, and maintainers of the building blocks of spiritual formation.

Personal Confessional Adherence and Academic Freedom

Evangelicals voluntarily, out of love for Christ, commit themselves to a pattern of belief and practice, and to uphold a series of key truths, helpfully summarized in four-fold fashion by David Bebbington in this way: (1) conversion as the definitive Christian experience; (2) the Bible as the revealed and authoritative Word of God and the basis for all Christian belief, practice and life; (3) the atoning death of Christ on the cross as the heart of the Christian message; and (4) a conviction that Christianity should be lived out in active service and witness.[5] Evangelicals take these fundamental truths and believe, cherish, defend, and live them out. It is an aspect of the love and service for Christ and his church for evangelicals to willingly and gladly embrace the yoke of doctrinal belief that brought them into the faith and has preserved them there in the midst of a community that shares the same values. These truths have provided a rock for their faith and witness through many challenges, and are not to be given up lightly.

However, in embarking on detailed academic study that pertains to these issues, they recognize there are challenges and perplexities. The evangelical faith is willingly accepted as a yoke for guidance and direction, but not a straightjacket that constrains and suffocates. Alongside these deeply held convictions, evangelicals are also committed to the principle of freedom of research, learning, and teaching. Their desire is not for a static faith, but instead to go deeper, think more clearly, and fearlessly and unequivocally state their findings. The evangelical student needs to be helped to live within this tension between openness and commitment.

Research Scholarship as Service to the Church

In his *Ecclesiastical Ordinances*, alongside the role of pastors, John Calvin also described the role of the teachers, or 'doctors' of the church (based on Ephesians 4:11). Their role was to instruct the believers in sound doctrine, and challenge ignorance or false opinions. The 'doctor of the church' was to provide aid and instruction for maintaining the doctrine of God, and also for defending the church from injury by the doctrinal failings of pastors and ministers. This was vital service to the church, and a great responsibility. However, this did not mean the doctor of the church was in any way superior to other leaders. The

5. D. Bebbington, *Evangelicalism in Modern Britain: A History from the 1730s to the 1980s* (London: Unwin Hyman, 1989), 5–17.

doctor of the church was to be subject like any other minister to ecclesiastical discipline, and the approval of other ministers was needed in the appointment.[6]

Evangelical scholars have come to believe that the deep and detailed study of the core matters of the Christian faith enjoined of the 'doctor of the church'– whether of biblical text, core theological statement, or an aspect of Christian practice – is not inimical to the maintenance of the historic Christian faith. As the 'General Principles Governing the Research Activity,' set for Tyndale House in 1944 assert: 'Error is manifold, but Truth is one, and those who, in dependence upon God Whose Word is Truth, set out to discover fresh Truth therefrom, are well assured that Truth can never be self-contradictory, but must always promote the glory of Him who says, "I am the Truth".'[7] On this basis, even evangelicals who hold most closely to the Reformed doctrine of Scripture are willing to undertake detailed scientific study of the text of the books that make up the canon. They gladly explore the context of thought and life in which the different books of Scripture were written, or in which doctrine was developed in the subsequent centuries. Scripture to them is a rich jewel with many sides which is to be held up and looked at from different perspectives, and in so doing its greater beauty is revealed. Evangelicals are desirous to preserve truth, while setting aside wrongful or unhelpful interpretations and emphases that have developed, in the belief that the integrity of the Christian message will be thereby affirmed and enhanced.

Those undertaking doctoral studies need considerable help to creatively navigate a way through these tensions. They need help to learn as evangelicals how to promote biblical, theological, historical, missiological and practical studies in a spirit of loving loyalty to the Christian faith as set out in Scripture, the Historical Creeds, and the Confessions of the Reformation. They also need a willingness to establish collaborative relationships with others engaged in similar research, such that evangelical scholarship can take its place at the forefront of Biblical and Theological Studies.

In my experience of supporting evangelical doctoral students in a range of contexts, I sadly find this is an area in which they receive little advice or help. They are looking for supervisors who will model integration and consistency in the 'openness and commitment' tension. I sometimes wonder about the reasons why this is lacking. Is there an assumption that students 'have got it all sorted', so supervisors don't need to discuss these issues? A surprising number of students of the biblical text do not even have a clearly formed doctrine of Scripture. Or, maybe, there is a reluctance by supervisors to open up about personal struggles and how they have been resolved (which might be seen as unduly

---

6. J. Calvin, 'Ecclesiastical Ordinances,' in *Theological Treatises*, ed. J. K. S. Reid, Library of Christian Classics (Philadelphia: The Westminster Press, 1954), 58–82, 333–343.

7. F. F. Bruce, D. Johnston, and L. Stephen-Hodge, 'General Principles Governing the Research Activity Tyndale House, 1944,' in *Research for the Academy and the Church: Tyndale House and Fellowship: The First Sixty Years*, ed. T. A. Noble (Leicester: IVP, 2006), 50–51.

directive, or a sign of weakness), with instead a preference only to talk in abstract terms about the issues raised. In my view, this reticence has not served evangelical doctoral students well.

Exercise

Write down a list of the 'openness and commitment' tensions you have found in your own scholarly discipline.

Beside each item on your list, write down how you have resolved those tensions.

Research Needs Humility

In the words of John Stott:

> We need the humility of Mary. She accepted God's purpose, saying, 'May it be to me as you have said' . . . We also need Mary's courage. She was so completely willing for God to fulfil his purpose, that she was ready to risk the stigma of being an unmarried mother, of being thought an adulteress herself and of bearing an illegitimate child. She surrendered her reputation to God's will. I sometimes wonder if the major cause of much theological liberalism is that some scholars care more about their reputation than about God's revelation. Finding it hard to be ridiculed for being naive and credulous enough to believe in miracles, they are tempted to sacrifice God's revelation on the altar of their own respectability. I do not say that they always do so. But I feel it right to make the point because I have myself felt the strength of this temptation.[8]

Some years ago, I was talking to a senior academic in the USA who reported to me his response to a question a theological student had asked him about how to serve God while doing a PhD. He replied simply, 'Teach Sunday school class. It will keep you rooted in serving the local church, and you will find children ask the most profound theological questions'.

---

8. John Stott, *The Authentic Jesus* (London: Marshalls, 1985), 66.

Research Should Be Done for the Glory of God

Christian supervisors need to demonstrate humility and appropriate scholarly caution about the findings of their research, and model this to students.

They need to show students how their scholarship will be tested and evaluated by others, and how this ongoing scholarly process of critical interaction should be welcomed and celebrated, even when this means earlier findings need to be re-evaluated or reworked.

The controlling desire of the researcher is to be the desire to bring glory to God through research, just as through any other part of Christian ministry. God alone should get all the credit for the insights he brings.

Reflective Questions

What is your strongest motivation in offering supervision to doctoral students?

How does your understanding of the task of the supervisor relate to the *missio Dei*?

What are the biggest barriers to research that your doctoral students will face?

Further Reading

Delamont, S., P. Atkinson, and O. Parry. *Supervising the PhD: A Guide to Success*. Bristol, PA: The Society for Research into Higher Education & Open University Press, 1997.

Eley, A., and R. Murray. *How to Be an Effective Supervisor*. Maidenhead: Open University Press, 2009.

Phillips, E. M., and D. S. Pugh. *How to Get a PhD: A Handbook for Students and their Supervisors*. Maidenhead: Open University Press, 2010. (Kindle edition available also.)

Quality Assurance Agency, *Doctoral Degree Characteristics*. www.qaa.ac.uk/en/Publications/ Documents/Doctoral_Characteristics.pdf

Shaw, I. *Best Practice Guidelines for Doctoral Programs*. Carlisle: Langham Global Library, 2015.

Smith, K. *Writing and Research: A Guide for Theological Students*. Carlisle: Langham Global Library, 2015

Taylor, Stan, and Nigel Beasley. *A Handbook for Doctoral Supervisors*. New York: Routledge, 2005.

Walker, G. E., C. M. Golde, L. Jones, A. C. Bueschel, and P. Hutchings. *The Formation of Scholars: Rethinking Doctoral Education for the Twenty-First Century*. San Francisco: Jossey-Bass, 2008.

Walker, M., and P. Thomson, eds. *The Routledge Doctoral Supervisor's companion: Supporting Effective Research in Education and the Social Sciences*. New York: Routledge, 2010.

Wisker, Gina. *The Good Supervisor: Supervising Postgraduate and Undergraduate Research for Doctoral Theses and Dissertations*. New York: Palgrave MacMillan, 2005.

3

'Do,' or 'Don't Do,' as Was Done unto You: Your Own PhD Journey

If you have successfully completed a PhD, you are a survivor! Congratulations!
Sadly many don't survive the process and the supervision experience. When I was doing my own PhD at a major research university in the UK in the early 1990s, the extraordinary statistic was published that at one of Britain's most elite universities more than 50 percent of those who started a PhD degree never completed it. The figures sent shock waves through the research establishment and many practices and approaches to research doctoral studies were subsequently changed and improved. Yet in 2012 the British newspaper *The Guardian* was still reporting a failure or non-completion rate of over 40 percent in many British universities, and that in the United States only 57 percent of doctoral students had achieved their PhD within ten years of starting their studies – in the humanities the completion figure was down to just 49 percent.[1] Such figures should make us pause and reflect on our approaches to doctoral students and supervision, and what might go wrong. Clearly, in many cases, things are not as they should be.

One significant trend as a result of these issues has been an increased emphasis on the whole process of doctoral education. There is a lot more needed to produce a research degree than simply being given a library card, access to a large pile of books, and occasional contact with a supervisor. The process of developing and writing a research project at doctoral level study needs to be thoroughly understood and clearly marked out. Doctoral studies thrive in a conducive environment – a research culture (see ch. 11 in this handbook).

We surely want our students to succeed. And our students have a right to the support, resources, and environment in order to do so. With the increased emphasis, especially

---

1. Daniel K. Sokol, 'Is a PhD the right option for you?' theguardian.com, Wednesday 12 September 2012.

in the litigious West, on the rights of the consumer, there needs to be a strong focus on quality assurance. Many will remember the case of Stella Liebeck who successfully sued the fast-food chain McDonalds for negligence after she spilled a cup of their scalding hot coffee on her leg. She asked for $20,000 to cover the medical treatment she needed, which McDonalds refused. In an object lesson to all corporate lawyers, when the matter went to court in New Mexico the jury instead awarded her $2.8 million dollars citing the negligence of the fast-food chain in serving coffee that was too hot, although the judge reduced the final payout. While McDonalds coffee is still apparently as hot as ever, we need to recognize that students who pay considerable sums in tuition fees and research costs are in one sense consumers, and have rights. Not only to be not served scalding hot coffee (!), but also to be treated fairly, have high quality facilities, good supervision, and all-in-all a positive experience – whether they pass or not. In an evangelical institution, this is not just a potential legal issue, but it is also a matter of treating our fellow believers with integrity, fairness, decency, and respect.

Supervisors who are committed to serving the Lord through providing doctoral supervision need to strive for excellence in all that they do – out of respect for our students, for our own professional reputation, and above all to honor God.

Yet, on the whole, even in some universities, there is limited training available in the area of supervision of doctoral students. There are some generic books (recommended in this handbook) which are helpful, but not all supervisors read them. In an absence of training, we tend often to fall back on our own experiences, and consciously, or sometimes unconsciously, we use them as a model.

When running training seminars for doctoral supervisors, I give each participant the opportunity to reflect on the best and worst part of the PhD supervision he or she received.

So here is your opportunity to do just that:

Reflective Questions

Think back to your overall experience of doing a doctorate (however many years back that was):

Was it on the whole a good experience, or on the whole not a good one?

Now, list the five best things about that experience.

Now list the five worst things.

Write down in a series of words some of the thoughts and emotions that come to mind when you think about your doctoral journey – such as challenging, expensive, etc.

If you had the opportunity again, what would you most like to change in your doctoral journey?

What would you most like to retain?

What lessons from your experience would you most like to share with the research students you will supervise?

My Own Experience of Being Supervised

As I reflect on my own experience of more than twenty years ago, the years spent doing my doctorate were some of the most enjoyable and fulfilling in my Christian ministry. I was working on a topic I was committed to and believed was highly relevant. My supervisor was interested in – I might even say 'excited by' – what I was discovering, but he was an old school Brit who did not do emotions in a big way! He took a personal interest in me, and regularly asked me about my family. I had access to world-class resources in terms of library and archives. While undertaking doctoral studies I was given some opportunities to present a few lectures, and seminars, and assist with marking. All the work I submitted for comment to my supervisor was read thoroughly, and detailed comments given. My supervisor graciously let me see some unpublished notes from his own research. There was a good relationship of professional respect and trust, which continued after I had completed my doctorate – he provided references for the job I eventually was given. I started doctoral studies as a part-time student while working in pastoral ministry, which I also loved, but I personally found it difficult to do justice to both church and studies. As the challenge deepened, I was blessed to receive a national research award. It was not generous, but it met my tuition fees and my family's basic needs and meant I was able to devote myself full-time to studies. I have much to praise God for about the process and experience.

Yet there were aspects of my PhD journey that were not ideal. The library where I worked had no designated study spaces for research students, so I had to carry all my books and notes with me to various locations – and doctoral students amass a lot of books! There was no research seminar in my subject area, and little sense of a research culture – although there were many other researchers working on faculty and doing doctoral studies.

Not everyone can recall having a good doctoral experience. Books such as *How to Get a PhD*[2] contain many instructive accounts of where things go wrong, and often this was because things did not work out with the supervisors.

---

2. E. M. Phillips and D. S. Pugh, *How to Get a PhD: A Handbook for Students and Their Supervisors* (Maidenhead: Open University Press, 2010).

Since completing my doctorate, I have regularly reflected with a large number of other doctoral students and doctoral graduates on their experience of being supervised in a wide range of contexts. When I run training for supervisors of students, I am always interested to hear the story of their experience and how it worked out. Below are some of the comments they have made over the years about things that were helpful, and not so helpful, and some experiences that were frankly terrible. Some were supervised in evangelical theological seminaries, and others in secular universities where not all supervisors were Christians. They are provided to illustrate the varied range of experiences it is possible for students to encounter in their doctoral studies. They are included without comment, but I am sure you will have your own observations about them! Many of the issues they raise are dealt with later in this handbook.

Comments from Doctoral Students as to What They Found Were Helpful Features of Supervision

- 'My supervisor was always available when I needed him.'
- 'My supervisor offered support and help in the early stages when I was trying to find direction.'
- 'I enjoyed being academically stretched by my supervisor.'
- 'I was encouraged by seeing my supervisor clearly enjoying my research topic and enthusiastically reading what I had written.'
- 'My supervisor asked me to share my new-found academic expertise with others.'
- 'She made sure I was connected to a church.'
- 'It was good to gain experience as a teaching assistant while doing doctoral studies.'
- 'I really enjoyed the privilege of detailed one to one conversations at peer academic level.'
- 'I valued being invited to my supervisors house with a group of other doctoral students.'
- 'My supervisor worked hard to help me secure research funding.'
- 'The knowledge of my supervisor was amazing.'
- 'I felt he was a very caring person.'
- 'Although a brilliant academic he was very down to earth.'
- 'She made sure I participated in the PhD Seminar.'
- 'I appreciated the prompt response to all work I submitted for comment.'
- 'The supervisor set clear expectations for a PhD: "Get a driver's license and then drive."'
- 'My supervisor helped me get articles published.'
- 'My supervisor invited me to co-author a project with her.'

Comments from Doctoral Students as to What They Found Were Unhelpful Features of Supervision

- 'My supervisor "dumped me" after two years saying he could no longer offer supervision, and told me to find another supervisor.'
- 'I got little response from my supervisor when I contacted him.'
- 'My supervisor makes the odd comment on my work and I have no idea if they have read large parts of the sections at all.'
- 'My supervisor did not seem interested in meeting me.'
- 'My supervisor made rude and insulting personal remarks to me.'[3]
- 'My supervisor was not up-to-date in his scholarship, and asked me to use sources and methods that were twenty years out of date. This meant my examiners made me make many corrections to the thesis.'
- 'Seminars were not controlled well, with irrelevant questions allowed.'
- 'An external professor from a well-known university was invited to give a research seminar, but he was semi-drunk, made crude jokes, and derogatory comments about the Bible in his talk, and no faculty member stopped him.'
- 'I had no idea how I was progressing – was I doing ok, or badly? The feedback given was so general I was "flying blind". I needed to know if my work was at doctoral level or not.'
- 'My supervisor did not help me with planning, or offering clear reachable goals. I felt constantly overwhelmed with the size of the project I had taken on.'
- 'After two years it was clear that I was never going to finish the project I had embarked on in the time allowed, and needed to scale it back. My supervisor was reluctant to allow this, and kept saying it will be fine. In the end I had to make the cuts without his support.'
- 'I received no encouragement to attend conferences and or submit work for publication.'
- 'He went off for long absences without telling me in advance.'
- 'I felt my supervisor was not caring.'
- 'She was business-like and remote.'
- 'The approach was just too controlling.'
- 'As soon as I encountered difficulties, my supervisor suggested I dropped out, rather than supporting me through them.'
- 'I did not know whether my supervisor was supporting and advising me, or assessing me ready to fail.'

---

3. This was in a secular university context, but wherever it happens such behavior is totally unprofessional and inexcusable, and is a justifiable cause for complaint, as happened in this circumstance. A move to an alternative supervisor was negotiated for this student.

- 'Anything I wrote or suggested that was outside the supervisor's range of experience was immediately dismissed by him.'

Reflective Questions

As you read the experiences of these students, both positive and negative, are there any things that personally stand out as areas you should address, enhance, or continue to do?

What were the five most helpful things your supervisor did?

What were the three least helpful things he or she did?

How can you avoid repeating those?

Finding a Model in Jesus

Write down a list of specific characteristics that Jesus showed as a teacher and mentor of his disciples?[4]

Based on this, what are the core attributes that you as a doctoral supervisor want to demonstrate?

What are the worst mistakes you want to avoid?

What is the best single impression you want to leave?

The Worst Possible Scenario

Here are the edited highlights, or should I say 'lowlights', of a disastrous doctoral journey as reported anonymously in the *Education Guardian*, 25 September 2001. It demonstrates almost every form of bad practice in doctoral supervision:

> In all the time he was a PhD student he met with his supervisor on no more than six occasions and discussed his work for a total of no more than two hours. He enrolled at the university only to find his supervisor had gone on a half-year sabbatical. The student went away on his own and wrote the first

---

4. Some answers given in discussion have included: Jesus did not withhold information; he modeled personally what he taught; he applied theory to practice; he was willing to confront error and wrong thinking; he allowed his disciples to try out false trails and make mistakes; his approach was relational; he explained difficult issues clearly; he prepared his disciples to take the ministry forward.

draft of his thesis in a year and sent it to the supervisor. On his return his supervisor said he had not read it. Twelve months later the supervisor agreed to read it, but only looked at the introduction and chapter 1, and made some very negative remarks. The student then re-edited the whole thesis and sent it in, but the supervisor never replied. He later learned that his supervisor had gone on sabbatical again, this time for a year. In his place an interim supervisor was appointed who had just gained his PhD. The student showed him his re-edited draft, and six months later it was returned with a few comments. On the basis of these, the thesis was then re-edited again and submitted for examination. After the examination date was set, the student was informed that the examiners had been changed from the ones originally agreed on, although he had not been asked or consulted about this. The exam was now conducted with examiners extremely hostile to his area of work and the argument he put forward. The thesis was, not surprisingly, deferred for major revisions. When the original supervisor returned from his absence, he said he could pull some strings to get the candidate an MPhil degree. The student refused this offer, and when the supervisor was not prepared to look at a further revision of the thesis, he completed the task entirely on his own and submitted it for re-examination. When he heard that this was being done, the supervisor refused to grant permission for the thesis to be examined, but the student pressed his case, appealed, was re-examined, and remarkably passed. Many months later the student was casually browsing the titles in a bookshop in his area of interest, and noticed a new one written by his supervisor. As he opened it and read it, he was astonished to find that it was a completely plagiarized version of his original thesis that the supervisor claimed not to have had time to read all those years before.

This is the most extreme case of gross professional misconduct. My prayer is that this was not your experience. In our supervision we must ensure that nothing remotely resembling such bad practice nature is ever repeated.

Case Study

James and John are two very able research students. They are being supervised by a new faculty member who has been very keen to take on research students, and he speaks often about how excited he is with the opportunity, and how he believes he can bring something new to the research process. As second supervisor of their doctoral research, you are not the main contact with the students, and your role is to provide general support and subject-specific guidance, but not take the main lead in their supervision. You meet James and John from time to time to see how their work is going, and at first they seem generally pleased, but then they begin to comment that it would be nice to see their main supervisor more often. After a year both James and John report on the regular student feedback forms that the institution sends out, that they would like more contact with their main supervisor, and to receive more detailed comments on their work. You decide to meet them about this, and although they do not wish to formally complain at how things are going, it becomes clear that they have only met their main supervisor twice in the last 6 months despite the fact that it is the early stages of their research. They feel that the main supervisor does not offer much comment on their written work, and he just says 'it is fine' when they ask for feedback. You ask to see a piece of work that has been submitted, on which you find that the main supervisor has only made a few comments here and there in the margins. James jokes, 'I sometimes wonder if he actually really reads what I submit.' You informally speak to the main supervisor about how things are going with the students, and he says they are both doing well and don't need much feedback or direction from him. When you probe a bit further he becomes more defensive and says that it is his style to encourage independence and not to 'crowd' the scholar, and then he starts to get a little animated and asserts 'it's their work after all.' After another two months, James says he is wondering about dropping out of the program.

Questions

What institutional issues does this raise?

What steps should you as second supervisor / reader take in this situation?

4

Developing Critical Thinking Skills: Building the Foundations for the Doctorate

According to the ICETE Beirut Benchmarks, the doctoral qualification will be awarded to students who have

> demonstrated their capacity for critical analysis, independent evaluation of primary and secondary source materials, and synthesis of new and inter-related ideas through coherent argumentation.[1]

To successfully complete a doctorate, students need to demonstrate high level and relevantly applied thinking skills in sustained pieces of written work.

Surface Learning and Deep Learning

Writers in the field of higher education have distinguished between 'surface learning', and 'deep learning'.[2]

Surface Learning

In this the 'learned' person is the teacher. The student memorizes and repeats what the teacher teaches. Learning is seen as students cramming large amounts of information into their minds, and then repeating it to satisfy their teacher or examiner. There is no necessity for the information to impact or change the student. The key educational skill being taught in 'surface learning' is recall of detail.

---

1. 'Beirut Benchmarks,' in Shaw, *Best Practice*, Section 1.

2. For example, Jackie Lublin, 'Deep, Surface and Strategic Approaches to Learning,' in *Good Practice in Teaching and Learning*, Training Document of Centre for Teaching and Learning: University College, Dublin, 2003; and 'Surface and Deep learning–University of Birmingham,' https://intranet.birmingham. ac.uk/as/cladls/edudev/documents/public/ebl/journey/surface-and-deep-learning.pdf.

This approach tends to produce a content-heavy curriculum. Students work hard, learning as much as they can from the 'learned' person at the front of the class. The approach discourages independence of learning, and produces heavy reliance on the teacher.

The result of this approach is that the students who do well are good at the recall of facts and details, but they are much less able to make connections and build hypotheses. Students learn to pass tests so that they can 'jump through the hoops' that the study institution requires them to, and are motivated by fear of failure.

Students trained in this context do well in a structured learning environment, and thrive on detailed and closely structured assessment procedures. However, they find they are ill-equipped to deal with the flexible, creative and original approaches that are at the center of advanced research, especially at doctoral level.

Deep Learning

While surface learning can provide information and knowledge useful for further study, 'deep learning' is of a different nature, and is more to do with developing the skills to understand, use, and apply information. Research students need to get beyond the bare facts, to make meaning of those facts, to connect knowledge and understanding. They need to have a more holistic approach, and move beyond grasping the smaller details to see the bigger picture. It is vital to see how findings relate to the wider academic discourse.

In deep learning emphasis is placed not just on increasing knowledge, but on shaping the thinking skills of a student. It becomes a way of making sense of the world through exploring a particular issue in detail. The student is encouraged to 'see' how something works.

This means that teachers stress the meaning and relevance of the subject matter. They encourage and empower students into independent thinking and making responsible choices. Students are motivated by interest in the subject, and a desire to know, understand, and apply what they learn, as opposed to just wanting to pass assessments.

From Knowledge to Understanding

In doctoral students, it is important to build the 'deep learning' skills that are core to independent critical thinking and research. The doctoral student needs to build from Knowledge to Understanding

The Knowledge Seeker

- Stores up facts and concepts
- Breaks down knowledge into sub-units

- Works in methodical ways through problems
- Puts significant store on information

The Understanding Seeker

- Makes links to other areas of knowledge
- Finds ways to restructure materials
- Synthesizes ideas and arguments
- Likes to get the 'whole picture'
- Searches for underlying structure and meaning
- Is intuitive as to solutions and outcomes

So both 'knowledge seeking', and 'understanding seeking' skills are vital for the doctoral student, but the skills progression must be towards an emphasis on seeking understanding.

A phrase sometimes used of the doctoral-level student is that of the 'self-managing learner'. That helpfully sums up the development in skills intended.

Critical Thinking / Reflective Judgment

In building deep thinking skills this capacity for critical thinking, or making independent analytical judgment, is crucial.

Experts in this field use the phrase 'critical thinking' in a *positive* sense, meaning 'a probing inquisitiveness, a keenness of mind, a zealous dedication to reason, and a hunger or eagerness for reliable information.'[3]

In some educational systems this is inculcated from an early age, but in others it is discouraged as disrespectful of teachers and traditions. In cultures where there is great deference and respect for the teacher, or the great thinkers of the past or even the present, the emphasis is on learning and lovingly reproducing their work. To such students, the skills of analysis and critical enquiry, do not come naturally. Asking profound questions about why something is written, and whether its assumptions are accurate, is not easy for them. In these cases, the supervisor needs to work hard to develop the abilities of students to demonstrate these new skills. Yet they are crucial to success at doctoral level.

Some may question the validity of this emphasis on independent critical thinking, arguing that it is a product of Greek philosophy, or from the Western Enlightenment. However, there is a strong case for arguing that the capacity for making independent reflective judgment, or undertaking critical analysis, is in fact a God-given capacity which the Christian is required to use. As a created capacity it therefore spans cultures and time.

---

3. P. A. Facione, '*Critical Thinking: What It Is and Why It Counts*,' www.insightassessment.com, 2015 update, 10.

A Biblical Case for Reflective Judgment

A God-Created Capacity

Straight after the act of creation, Adam and Eve are asked to use their reflective judgment in a response of obedience to the Creator's commands – Genesis 2:15–17. The consequences of a right or wrong choice are presented to them, but they are invited to use the reflective judgment with which they have been created. Tragically the judgment they make is the wrong one, with terrible consequences. The account indicates that the capacity for reasoned decision and choice was there before the fall. The problem is not with the capacity, but the failure to use it properly to test out the faulty information provided by the tempter. Although in a fallen world the ability to make a reflective judgment is now thoroughly flawed, it still remains an important aspect of the created order.

Wisdom

Wisdom is celebrated in Scripture, but it has to be learned, and must be associated with faith – 'The fear of the LORD is the beginning of wisdom' (Prov 9:10). Wisdom needs to be used well in both spiritual and non-spiritual contexts. Solomon asked God for wisdom, and used it well in the case of the two mothers and the babies (1 Kgs 3:16–28). Tragically, he did not use it well in his choice of marriage partners, including women who worshiped foreign gods, and thereby undermined the worship of the nation which was designed to be exclusive to God.

Reflective Judgment and Wise Counsel

A key figure in the court of David was Ahithophel, renowned for his wise counsel. When Absalom invited him to take up his cause, it was of such concern to David that he encouraged Hushai the Arkite to offer his services to Absalom as another counsellor to thwart his advice (2 Sam 15). As a result, Absalom's decision-making radar is jammed by Hushai's contrary advice. Reflective judgment involves deciding between competing voices: its exercise is a contested area.

Reflective Judgment Counters Over-Emotional or Prejudiced Decision Making

A further instructive example occurs after the death of Solomon when the complaints of the people are presented to his son Rehoboam by Jeroboam (1 Kgs 12). Rehoboam seeks counsel from Solomon's former advisors, and then from the young men of the court, after which he needs to make a reflective decision on what he hears. Again, the choice is a flawed one, spurred by the impulsive excitement and emotion engendered by his peer group, not by the evidence. Doctoral students need to weigh often conflicting information carefully, and to come to a decision based on the evidence, not emotion.

The Christian's Reflective Judgment Is Biblically Informed

An added dimension to the evangelical Christian's use of reflective judgment is given in the New Testament when the Apostle Paul visits Berea. This occurs straight after his rejection at Thessalonica (Acts 17:2–3), where he 'reasoned with them from the Scriptures,' while 'explaining and proving that the Christ had to suffer and rise from the dead.' Although some were persuaded by the way Paul presents the biblical arguments, other Thessalonians violently rejected Paul's message. The reception at Berea is quite different. Here Paul and Silas were received 'with great eagerness,' but the Bereans use their reflective judgment before deciding how they would respond to the message. So they carefully test what the Apostle says, examining the Scriptures every day to see if what Paul said 'was true.' Biblically-informed reflective judgment is deployed with a positive outcome.

Reflective Judgment Should Be Honed and Applied in Community

The community dimension in the use of reflective judgment is shown in Acts 15. Here the difficult issue of incorporating Gentile converts into the church is debated. The different sides offer their viewpoints, and the evidence is weighed in the light of Scripture, before James offers a summary on the part of the apostles. This highlights the importance of debate and dialogue in the (scholarly) community, the value of weighing different perspectives, and exploring their consequences. In this situation, God-given, creative use of rationality to come to reflective judgment is paramount at a pivotal moment for the church.

God-Given Capacities Need to Be Used in a Deep and Applied Way

From what we read in the Scripture, the capacity for independent, critical thinking, is a God-given capacity from creation, and the Christian is called to use it rightfully. It is actively deployed (not always well) by believers in both the Old and New Testaments. Asking students from cultures where this is less prominent in the educational system to create an original piece of research work based on the use of critical thinking is therefore not imposing on them a Greek, or Western-Enlightenment method, but rather liberating them to use what is a God-given capacity. The tools and methods by which reflective judgment is employed may well have been developed in the Western world, such as Socratic questioning, syllogistic reasoning, or the Hegelian dialectic approach, but they build on the created capacity. The evangelical Christian is therefore able to use their redeemed mind, illuminated by the Spirit, to deploy their critical reasoning capacity in a biblically and theologically informed way as an aspect of loving God with 'heart, soul, and mind'.

Indeed, the contrast with those who refuse to use this God-given capacity is notable. Those who reject the Bible's message are often condemned as 'unreasoning' animals – 2 Peter 2:12; Jude 10; Acts 19:9.

Critical reflection is therefore an aspect of the daily Christian disciplines: we are called to read, correctly interpret, and apply the Scriptures to everyday life situations, and guard against extreme, fanatical, or erroneous, interpretations both by ourselves and on the part of others. An unreasoning Christian, blindly obeying the dictates of some external authority, or the impulse of each and every emotion, is not in a good place.

This means that enhancing the capacity for independent reflective judgment is not just something asked of doctoral students alone. It should be encouraged so that all Christians are driven afresh to the Scriptures – to think, explore, and deepen their faith. They become active learners, not just unthinking and passive. Reflective judgment enables Christians to make informed decisions, without following blindly the dictates of a religious leader, it gives them the capacity to **interpret and apply** the Scriptures in everyday contexts – at home and work – without the need for constant spiritual direction. It fosters integration of faith and life.

In the view of one major educational study, reflective judgment means that in decisions over what to believe or do, reasoned consideration is given to 'evidence, context, methods, standards, and conceptualizations'[4]

So Christian doctoral students are being asked to excise an ability that Christians at all levels should demonstrate, but at a higher level, and with a greater degree of academic sophistication.

Critical Thinking Is a Guard for Faith and Society

Throughout history there have regularly been assaults on learning, whether by book burning, the exile of intellectuals, or regulations aimed at suppressing freedom of research. They attempt to frustrate the fair-minded, evidence-based, and unfettered pursuit of knowledge. Many totalitarian regimes have based their educational systems on mis-information about the past, or refusal to allow those facts to be studied.

This means that societies should place a very high value on critical thinking. The landmark 1990 Delphi Report in the USA set out the findings of a two year project to articulate an international expert consensus on critical thinking, including its core cognitive skills. The experts identified the characteristics of an ideal critical thinker,

---

4. *The APA Delphi Report, Critical Thinking: A Statement of Expert Consensus for Purposes of Educational Assessment and Instruction*, 1990 ERIC Doc. No: ED, 315–423.

and presented a series of recommendations relating to critical thinking instruction and assessment.

The Delphi Report[5] defined critical thinking as,

> purposeful, self-regulatory judgment which results in interpretation, analysis, evaluation, and inference, as well as explanation of the evidential, conceptual, methodological, criteriological, or contextual considerations upon which that judgment is based. Critical Thinking is essential as a tool of inquiry. As such, Critical Thinking is a liberating force in education and a powerful resource in one's personal and civic life. While not synonymous with good thinking, Critical Thinking is a pervasive and self-rectifying human phenomenon.

They specifically defined the ideal critical thinker as,

> habitually inquisitive, well-informed, trustful of reason, open minded, flexible, fair-minded in evaluation, honest in facing personal biases, prudent in making judgments, willing to reconsider, clear about issues, orderly in complex matters, diligent in seeking relevant information, reasonable in the selection of criteria, focused in inquiry, and persistent in seeking results which are as precise as the subject and the circumstances of inquiry permit.

Educating good critical thinkers assists wider society in 'working toward this ideal.'

Key Skills and Approaches in Developing Critical Thinking

The Delphi Report identified a series of skills considered essential to critical thinking, together with a related series of sub-skills:[6]

Skill	Sub-Skills	Related Questions
1. Interpretation	Categorization	How do we characterize / categorize this?
	Decoding Significance	How do we understand this event / experience / statement in this context?
	Clarifying Meaning	What meaning can be attributed to what was said / done?
	Related Questions	How does context inform this?
		How do we interpret this statement / issue?
		Where might this lead?

---

5. P. A. Facione, *Critical Thinking: A Statement of Expert Consensus for Purposes of Educational Assessment and Instruction, Executive Summary, 'The Delphi Report'* (The California Academic Press, Millbrae, 1990).
6. 'APA Delphi Report,' in *Critical Thinking*, ed. Facione, www.insightassessment.com, 2015 update, 10.

Skill	Sub-Skills	Related Questions
2. Analysis	Examining Ideas	Why does a person think that way?
	Identifying Arguments	What are the arguments for and against?
	Analysing Arguments	What lies behind the argument / idea?
		How do these arguments affect the conclusion?
3. Evaluation	Assessing Claims	Is the person sound / trustworthy in their judgment?
	Assessing Arguments	Are the arguments clear enough / powerful enough?
		Are the facts right?
		Is the conclusion reliable?
4. Inference	Questioning Evidence	What can be implied from the evidence?
		What more do we need to know?
		What problems can be foreseen with this argument / approach?
	Suggesting Alternatives	Is there another explanation?
		Are the assumptions on which this is based right?
		Are there other alternatives to consider?
	Building Conclusions	What are the outcomes if this argument / policy is followed through?
		Where do the assumptions take us?
5. Explanation	Stating Results	What was found?
		What was not found?
	Justifying Procedures	How were the results obtained?
		How was the interpretation arrived at?
	Presenting Arguments	Does the argument build logically step-by-step?
		Has the answer / decision been explained clearly?
		What made the writer think that was the right answer?
		Does the conclusion flow from the argument?
		Has the writer adequately explained their conclusion?
6. Self-Regulation	Self-Examination	How good is the evidence presented in the case?
		Can it be improved on?
		Was the methodology appropriate?
		How can conflicting evidence be reconciled?
	Self-Correction	Is anything missing?
		Are the conclusions convincing?

Personal Qualities Needed in Critical Thinkers

A series of aspects of the personal character disposition towards critical thinking in students have been identified. These serve as a useful outline of the intellectual virtues to develop among students at masters level prior to starting doctoral level work, and to nurture further in doctoral students, which are vital in growth towards academic maturity:

  i)   commitment to truth-seeking,
  ii) open-mindedness,
  iii) analytical ability,
  iv) ability to systematize,
  v)   willingness to ask key questions,
  vi) self-confidence.

In the light of these studies many colleges and universities introduced critical thinking courses to help develop these vital skills.

The Wider Transferable Value of Critical Thinking

This was the advice of The Chairman of the Joint Chiefs of Staff about the value of critical thinking, made in his commencement address to a graduating class of military officers:

> You will recall how you were inspired to **think critically** and to question without fear . . . to read widely and deeply, and to examine without end and grow intellectually . . . What I ask is this: pass it on.[7]

Some Key Aspects

Students need to recognize that the world is a complex place, that problems are real, and not easily solved. Realizing this helps develop a more balanced, and well-rounded person. The capacity for wise thinking should be extended to all aspects of life and conduct. Students who are critical thinkers will be equipped with advanced tools to handle the perplexities of life and Christian ministry.

It is no surprise that many with doctoral qualifications find themselves asked to take on strategic leadership roles. The training they have received has meant that their critical thinking skills have been sharpened and developed.

Resisting the Destructive Critical Impulse

One of the criticisms of critical thinking is that it produces Christians who question everything, and doubt everything. Is this necessarily going to happen?

---

7. Mike Mullen, 'Navy Admiral,' 11 June 2009, quoted in Facione, *Critical Thinking*, 1.

The answer is no. Christians are seekers after truth, not doubt. There is 'truth', which resides in God and needs to be explored, and that is what we are seeking. Indeed this is enormously profound. In searching for the 'truth' on a particular issue, we are exploring aspects of the mind and workings of God. The evangelical Christian who is a critical thinker will

    i)   Recognize that a problem exists and discuss that in their research proposal / thesis statement

    ii) Recognize that there is evidence, 'sources,' that need to be considered, including the Bible and key primary texts

    iii) Recognize that God has given us minds with which to tackle and propose answers to problems

Critical thinking is therefore about being 'open minded without being wishy-washy'. It is analytical without being nitpicky. Critical thinkers can be decisive without being stubborn, evaluative without being judgmental, and forceful without being opinionated'.[8]

Good Reflective Thinkers Say

    i)   'I hate it when people just give their opinions without reasons.'

    ii) 'You should not make a decision until other options have been considered.'

    iii) 'I like to read the original source myself, not just someone's summary of it.'

    iv) 'I like it when an issue is stated clearly.'

    v) 'It is good when complex arguments are presented in an orderly way.'

    vi) 'I appreciate how the information has been put together, with detail, but without losing sight of the big picture.'

    vii) 'I liked the balanced way the author approaches the issues.'

Poor Critical Thinkers Say

    i)   'I don't waste time checking what other writers have said.'

    ii) 'I just prefer to get the answers, without wading through the evidence and reasons that lie behind it.'

    iii) 'I am sincere in what I believe, so evidence is not important one way or the other.'

Recognizing the Process

Developing critical thinking skills takes time, and does not stop, even when a doctorate has been gained.

---

8. Facione, *Critical Thinking*, 25.

Further Reading

The APA Delphi Report, Critical Thinking: A Statement of Expert Consensus for Purposes of Educational Assessment and Instruction, 1990 ERIC Doc. No: ED 315–423.

Cottrell, S. *Critical Thinking Skills: Developing Effective Analysis and Argument*, 2nd Edition. Basingstoke: Palgrave, Macmillan, 2011.

———. *The Study Skills Handbook,* 4th edition. Basingstoke: Palgrave, Macmillan, 2013.

Facione, P. A. *Critical Thinking: What It Is and Why It Counts.* www.insightassessment.com, 2015 update, p. 10.

———. *Critical Thinking: A Statement of Expert Consensus for Purposes of Educational Assessment and Instruction, Executive Summary, 'The Delphi Report.'* Millbrae, CA: The California Academic Press, 1990.

Lublin, J. 'Deep, Surface and Strategic Approaches to Learning.' In *Good Practice in Teaching and Learning*, Training Document of Centre for Teaching and Learning: University College, Dublin, 2003; and 'Surface and Deep Learning–University of Birmingham,' https://intranet. birmingham.ac.uk/as/cladls/edudev/documents/public/ebl/journey/surface-and-deep-learning.pdf.

Murray, R. *How to Write a Thesis*, 2nd edition. Maidenhead: Open University Press, 2006

Paul, R., and L. Elder. *The Miniature Guide for Those Who Teach on How to Improve Student Learning: 30 Practical Ideas.* Dillon Beach, CA: Foundation for Critical Thinking Press, 2003.

———. *The Miniature Guide to the Art of Asking Essential Questions.* Dillon Beach, CA: Foundation for Critical Thinking Press, 2005.

———. *The Miniature Guide to Critical Thinking Concepts and Tools.* Dillon Beach, CA: Foundation for Critical Thinking Press, 2009.

Smith, K. *Writing and Research: A Guide for Theological Students.* Carlisle: Langham Global Library, 2015

Torrance, M., and G. Thomas. 'The Development of Writing Skills in Doctoral Research Students.' In *Postgraduate Education and Training in the Social Sciences. Processes and Products*, edited by R. G. Burgess, 105–123. London: Jessica Kingsley, 1994.

5

Building Critical Skills at Masters Level

Academic learning is based on the concept of skills progression, so it is important to understand what are the differences in skill levels between postgraduate masters level work, and those needed in doctoral-level work. Once that is understood, we need to develop ways of teaching these new skills and abilities. Clearly, much of this work should be done before doctoral studies start, indeed if students have not already begun to demonstrate at postgraduate masters level the skills they need to show at doctoral level they should not be admitted into a doctoral program.

As the student progresses through the academic levels, a greater emphasis is placed on independent learning, and the capacity to form independent opinions. Ultimately, in the final thesis / dissertation written at the doctoral level, students are required to demonstrate a capacity for original research and make an original contribution to knowledge.

Reflective Questions

What aspects did you find most different between masters-level and doctoral-level study in your subject-specialist area?

In what ways did your masters studies prepare you for doctoral-level study?

In what ways did masters-level studies not prepare you for doctoral-level study?

Masters Benchmarks

The European Bologna Process has set out the key skills considered to be needed at masters level in a series of benchmark statements.[1] The following is a summary.

---

1. www.qaa.ac.uk/en/Publications/.../Masters-degree-characteristics.pd, Appendix 2a: Descriptor for a higher education qualification at level 7: Master's degree.

Master's Degrees Are Awarded to Students Who Have Demonstrated:

- a systematic understanding of knowledge at the forefront of the discipline
- awareness of current issues at the forefront of their academic discipline
- comprehensive understanding of techniques that relate to their research, and how they are used to create and interpret knowledge
- evidence of originality in applying knowledge and tackling problems
- advanced conceptual understanding
- ability to evaluate advanced scholarship in the discipline
- ability to evaluate and critique methodologies
- ability to show originality in the application of knowledge in new or unfamiliar context

As a Result of Masters-Level Study, Students Should Be Able To:

- deal with complex issues both systematically and creatively
- make sound judgments in the absence of complete data
- communicate their conclusions clearly
- demonstrate self-direction in solving problems
- act autonomously in planning and implementing tasks
- continue to advance their knowledge and understanding
- exercise initiative and personal responsibility
- demonstrate independent learning ability
- understand how the boundaries of knowledge are advanced through research
- formulate judgments based on incomplete or limited information
- show personal responsibility and initiative, in complex and unpredictable professional environments.

Reflective Questions

Underline the key words in the above lists.

What do they mean?

List the key skills needed at doctoral level which need to have been demonstrated at masters level.

How should assessments of work conducted at masters level be framed so that they encourage self-directed learning?

Skills for Professional Contexts

Many masters courses are taken by professionals wishing to deepen their knowledge and understanding, but also increase their skill in decision making. For this reason, developing skills at masters level in how to make independent judgments is very important. Just as there are often no simple 'yes or no' answers to many academic questions, so too in professional contexts students need to find a way to resolve issues that have many perspectives without being overwhelmed by them. Otherwise they won't be able to make a decision for themselves.

Much of the study undertaken for master's degrees should therefore be at the forefront of an academic or professional discipline.

Developing Core Skills

1) Knowledge

One of the key needs of doctoral students is high levels of knowledge at the forefront of the discipline. The *ICETE Beirut Benchmarks for Research Doctoral Students* expresses this in terms of showing '**breadth of systematic understanding**', and producing work that '**extends the frontiers of knowledge**'.

Knowledge at the forefront of the discipline can be gained through good teaching and extensive reading, and for this lecturers are needed who are well-informed as to the latest scholarship in the field, and who are research-active. But there is more to getting a doctorate than learning a huge amount of facts and information.

Helping students to demonstrate 'breadth of systematic understanding' means instilling in them the ability not just to learn and repeat information, but to understand what it means. Therefore 'surface' learning approaches in the level just before the doctoral thesis – postgraduate masters, or even the coursework stage of a doctoral degree – that simply require students to learn material from lectures, handouts, and books and repeat them in essays, exams, or multiple choice questions will only serve to build a bank of information-type knowledge. This may have value in earlier academic levels, but in itself is not sufficient at masters level or in preparing students for doctoral level. Assessments based around simply reproducing knowledge are not good ways of developing the skills necessary for writing a doctoral-level thesis.

2) Understanding

Knowledge needs to be connected to understanding. It is one thing to know about an issue or problem, but another to understand how it works, or the reasons for it. Understanding, when it has been gained, can be applied in solving problems, evaluating difficulties, and proposing new approaches.

Understanding comes from the process of subjecting a body of information [knowledge], to reasoning skills, enquiry, synthesis, and application. We need to work hard to construct understanding from a range of evidence, which needs to be tested and evaluated. Once it is established it remains valid until other evidence or conclusions come along.

The basis of information, and approaches, upon which a discipline is based, are subject to change over time. At masters level students need to learn the skill of understanding, which enables them to meaningfully handle and employ information, and then maintain a mode of continuous learning and professional development so that they are aware of the changes and why they are taking place. Students need to be taught ways to reflect critically on the thoughts of others. But they also need to be able to reflect critically on their own thoughts and practice – to be actively reflective practitioners.

For the lecturer teaching at postgraduate masters level, this means much more than simply getting the student to replicate the way you think. Students need to develop their own independent capacities and approaches to think through issues. It may be comforting when you hear students repeating your ideas and approaches in classes and seminars, but advanced-level thinking needs to be integrated with their own background, their context, their culture, their experience, their personalities. It needs to be owned and integrated as their own thought. The lecturer needs to open up his or her approaches to critical evaluation, and not feel threatened when that takes place.

The Critical Thinking Skills to Develop

i)   **The inquisitive mind** – this provides an impetus in the search for knowledge. It recognizes that we can't be certain about some things, that problems exist, and hard work needs to be done to resolve them. For some masters and doctoral students, the inquisitive mind needs to be kept in check, so projects developed are not too large. For others it is a case of 'permission to think and be inquisitive'.

ii) **Capacity and confidence** – so that students are able to make defendable judgments based on high levels of knowledge and understanding.

iii) **Discernment** – Students need to recognize that in academic discourse on a subject there are many complex issues, and there might not be a clear right, or wrong answer to problems.

iv) **Interpretative skills** – judgments need to be based on skills of interpreting evidence.

v) **Responsibility** – Students need to appreciate that decisions have significant consequences and need to be taken with responsibility. Students are not playing an 'academic game' in the theological disciplines – issues studied are significant for the church and important to many believers.

vi) **Openness** – Students need to be aware that findings are always open to re-evaluation by others – the debate may never fully be closed.

Exercise

Get students to read a 'controversial' book in your subject area.

Ask them in a sentence or two to say what they felt about the book. Take some of the key words they use, and get them to produce a statement of response, for example, 'I found the book well argued, or thought provoking, or unconvincing.' Then get them to define what they mean by the terms they used. What constitutes a 'good' or 'convincing' argument'?

Other Exercises to Help Students Develop Critical Thinking Skills

i) Get students to read a key document or statement. Ask them to identify which is the most significant part of the statement or argument within it. Then get them to state why that is significant.

ii) Ask students to define the difference between making an assertion, and developing an argument. Get them to find examples of each.

iii) Get students to look at examples of their own work. Alongside the information being conveyed, what argument are they making? Why are they making that argument? How has it been developed and justified?

Handling Evidence

Some of the ablest proponents of critical thinking are lawyers in court. They use reason to try to convince the judge and jury of their client's case. They offer their own evidence and evaluate the significance of the evidence presented by the opposition lawyers through rigorous questioning of it. They analyze and evaluate the arguments advanced by the other side, and offer interpretations of the evidence.

Exercises

1) Create a class exercise that requires two students to present a key issue in your discipline in the form of a court case – with class members taking the part of key thinkers who are interviewed – give testimonies, and offer arguments for and against. Get students to use the skills of cross-examination and analysis before the class 'jury' comes to a verdict. Jury members can then debate the verdict, and be interviewed about how they decided to vote in the way they did. How did their ideas change during the debate?

2) Now create another class exercise which deals with a key 'problem' in your subject area. This time the students need to analyze the problem, and through collaboration, offer a solution.

Gauging the Level: Identifying Different Types of Writing

Students need to be able to identify different types of writing, and their significance for academic study. These can be summarized as:

i) **Descriptive writing** – the writer simply produces a record of what they have found

ii) **Descriptive reflection** – a description of evidence, with some reflection made, but this tends to be a personal value judgment

iii) **Dialogic reflection** – some reflection based on the literature, but tends to be based on one source / dialogue partner

iv) **Critical reflection** – a rounded exploration of reasons and approaches and underlying assumptions, including assessment of wider influences such as social and historical contextual factors

---

Class Exercise

Present students with a series of pieces of writing from the four categories above.

Get them to identify which types of writing they are, and the issues they raise.

Critically Analysing Texts

Critical analysis of key texts in the research field is a central part of postgraduate study. It enables the student to understand the 'state of the art' scholarship, and to set their own research in the context of the current academic discourse in their field.

Questions Students Should Ask When Critically Analysing Key Texts (Primary or Secondary)

i)   How far is the evidence appropriate for the argument? Is it reliable and useful?

ii)   Does the evidence support the conclusion? Is it strong enough?

iii)   Which pieces of evidence did you find most convincing?

iv)   In a sentence what are the bare-bones of the argument?

v)   Are the points made logically and sequentially? Could the order of the points have been improved?

vi)   Can you identify bias or assumptions behind the argument – does the author have a hidden agenda? Give examples.

vii)   What information is missing?

viii)   Do you agree with the author? If not, why not?

Applying These Skills in Postgraduate Writing

- Students need to learn to apply the same rigor to their own writing as they do when analysing the source materials of others.
- Help students to identify what their conclusion is likely to be after they have completed their research and before they start writing.
- Make sure students plan their work, and show how each section leads to the conclusion.

- Get students to keep referring back to this plan as they build each point to the conclusion to ensure that all of their writing leads towards it.
- Ensure each key point, and the conclusion, is supported by evidence. If there is not enough evidence to support the position, the student may need to change their conclusion.[2]

Ideas for Creating a Critically Reflective Learning Culture

i)   Create a relaxed, friendly, non-threatening environment in which issues can be debated, and views thoughtfully expressed, adapted, and changed.

ii) Don't overload students with content-based learning, and assessments that involve spending a lot of time in learning content in preparation for exams or other written assessments. Overloaded students will revert to surface learning approaches to 'get through'.

iii) Create practice exercises in which students are required to build the stages of an argument, rather than just the answer.

iv) Support the views of those who are at the early stages of their thinking, but create a framework where they are able to think again.

v)   Gently push students to question the assumptions that lie behind their statements. Make students give reasons for the opinions they express in debate. Make sure students are introduced to the 'problem areas' in their discipline at undergraduate or early postgraduate levels.

vi) Create assignments or classroom exercises that encourage students to see and debate issues from different sides, including those they don't agree with. Create opportunities where students need to actually come to a decision on an issue (e.g. class debates and discussions) with a vote.

vii) Develop assignments where students don't just explore the ideas of others, but need to argue to their own interpretation.

viii) Encourage students to go on debating issues out of class and over coffee.

ix) Encourage students to produce reflective journals in which they record the development and progression of their ideas.

---

2. For more detailed discussion and examples See S. Cottrell, *Critical Thinking Skills: Developing Effective Analysis and Argument*, 2nd Edition (Basingstoke: Palgrave, Macmillan, 2011); and S. Cottrell, *The Study Skills Handbook,* 4th Edition (Basingstoke: Palgrave, Macmillan, 2013).

x)   Recognize that in a class different scholars will be at different stages of developing critical thinking skills.

xi)   Design assessments that require integration of learning and subject areas, e.g. creating synoptic assignments that cover a range of issues or even disciplines. Use a variety of assessment formats.

xii)   Increase independent learning with decreased dependence on lecturer / tutor input. For example, allow elements of choice in assessments, or get students to develop their own title, which allows greater student engagement and ownership.

xiii) Ensure students evaluate the strengths and weaknesses of their own work and conclusions – 'if you were grading your own work, what grade would you give it? Why?'

xiv)   When assessments include reflection on a personal and professional practice, make sure students maintain a controlled critical distance from their own context and work.

xv)   Create opportunities at masters level for cohort-led learning; student-led presentations and seminars.

xvi)   Provide training in research skills and key methodology.

xvii) Give students experience of independent academic enquiry, and how to construct research proposals before they reach doctoral level.

xviii) Ensure students write a sustained dissertation / project of at least 15,000 words based on sustained research work.

xix)   Enable students to identify areas where they would like to do further research.

Some Key Intellectual Standards in Developing Critical Thinking[3]

Clarity: Unclear statements and questions make thinking about them difficult. Supplementary Questions include: *Could you elaborate further about that? Could you give an example or illustration of what you mean?*

---

3. For these and other ideas see R. Paul and L. Elder, *The Miniature Guide for Those Who Teach on How to Improve Student Learning: 30 Practical Ideas* (Dillon Beach, CA: Foundation for Critical Thinking Press, 2003); R. Paul and L. Elder, *The Miniature Guide to the Art of Asking Essential Questions* (Dillon Beach, CA: Foundation for Critical Thinking Press, 2005); R. Paul and L. Elder, *The Miniature Guide to Critical Thinking Concepts and Tools* (Dillon Beach, CA: Foundation for Critical Thinking Press, 2009).

Accuracy: A statement may be clear, but not accurate. *What is the evidence for this? How could we check on or verify that?*

Precision: A statement may be clear and accurate, but not precise enough to help our thinking. *Could you be more specific? Can you give a few more details?*

Relevance: A statement may be clear, accurate, precise, but not relevant to the issues being addressed. *How does that relate to the issue? How does that help us with this issue?*

Depth: A statement may be clear, true, precise, relevant, but simplistic or superficial. *How does this help us with the complexities of the issue or problem? Are we dealing with the most significant aspects of the issue?*

Breadth: A statement may be clear, true, precise, relevant, and have depth, but not take into account other legitimate perspectives or concerns. It may make sense to us, but not persuade others. *Do we need to look at this from a different perspective? How might others view this?*

Logic: A statement may contain information that is clear, true, precise, relevant, have both depth and breadth, but lack clear organization and flow (logic). *Does this make sense? Does that follow from what you said earlier? Do the conclusions follow from the evidence and argument?*

Fairness: An argument may make sense to us due to our commitments and biases. Are we being fair in our assessment of the evidence and argument, the views of others? Are we prepared to rethink our views? *Am I sympathetically considering the views of others?*

Some Spiritual Virtues That Should Accompany Critical Thinking

We need to be on our guard lest growth in critical thinking skills leads to pride, arrogance, or even the abuse of others and the views they hold. As we cultivate critical thinking we should also pursue the following:

Intellectual humility (as opposed to arrogance): We need to be conscious of the limits of our own knowledge and understanding, and aware of our own bias. The Christian scholar should not be claiming more than they actually know. Not boastful or conceited.

Intellectual courage (as opposed to cowardice): Willingness to listen to, and understand, beliefs and viewpoints that I, or my group, do not agree with. Not passively and uncritically accepting what we have been told. Courage to disagree with others when we have good biblical or intellectual reasons for doing so.

Intellectual empathy (as opposed to narrow-mindedness): A willingness to put myself in the place of others and see things from their perspective so that I might better understand them (even if I still disagree). A willingness to accept that sometimes we are wrong (also a dimension of humility).

Intellectual autonomy (as opposed to conformity): Learning to think for yourself, make your own assessments, analyze and evaluate on the basis of reason and evidence.

Intellectual integrity (as opposed to hypocrisy): Being true to your own thoughts and conclusions. Making your practice consistent with what you advise others to believe and do, and acknowledging where there are inconsistencies.

Intellectual perseverance (as opposed to laziness): Willingness to pursue difficult issues in the face of intellectual challenges or criticism. Refusing to draw conclusions under pressure from others, but basing them on the evidence, and wise judgment. Sometimes leaving issues aside until we get greater clarity.

'Fairmindedness' (as opposed to unfairness): Treating each viewpoint fairly, without resorting to personal feelings or prejudices, or those of my group. Refusing to seek just my own (or my group's) advantage, but instead seeking the good of all.

Intellectual grace (as opposed to judgmentalism): Exercising gentleness in how I disagree with others, and seeking to help them to come to better conclusions. Caring for the spiritual and intellectual well being of the other person, not just desiring to win a debate / argument.

Further Reading

The APA Delphi Report, Critical Thinking: A Statement of Expert Consensus for Purposes of Educational Assessment and Instruction, 1990 ERIC Doc. No: ED, 315–423.

Cottrell, S. Critical Thinking Skills: Developing Effective Analysis and Argument, 2nd Edition. Basingstoke: Palgrave, Macmillan, 2011.

———. The Study Skills Handbook, 4th edition. Basingstoke: Palgrave, Macmillan, 2013.

Facione, P. A. Critical Thinking: What It Is and Why It Counts. www.insightassessment.com, 2015 update, p. 10.

———. Critical Thinking: A Statement of Expert Consensus for Purposes of Educational Assessment and Instruction, Executive Summary, 'The Delphi Report.' Millbrae, CA: The California Academic Press, 1990.

Lublin, J. 'Deep, Surface and Strategic Approaches to Learning.' In Good Practice in Teaching and Learning, Training Document of Centre for Teaching and Learning: University College, Dublin, 2003; and 'Surface and Deep Learning–University of Birmingham,' https://intranet.

birmingham.ac.uk/as/cladls/edudev/documents/public/ebl/journey/surface-and-deep-learning.pdf.

Murray, R. *How to Write a Thesis*. Maidenhead: Open University Press, 2nd edition, 2006

Paul, R., and L. Elder. *The Miniature Guide for Those Who Teach on How to Improve Student Learning: 30 Practical Ideas*. Dillon Beach, CA: Foundation for Critical Thinking Press, 2003.

———. *The Miniature Guide to the Art of Asking Essential Questions*. Dillon Beach, CA: Foundation for Critical Thinking Press, 2005.

———. *The Miniature Guide to Critical Thinking Concepts and Tools*. Dillon Beach, CA: Foundation for Critical Thinking Press, 2009.

Smith, K. *Writing and Research: A Guide for Theological Students*. Carlisle: Langham Global Library, 2015.

Torrance, M., and G. Thomas. 'The Development of Writing Skills in Doctoral Research Students.' In *Postgraduate Education and Training in the Social Sciences. Processes and Products*, edited by R. G. Burgess, 105–123. London: Jessica Kingsley, 1984.

6

Helping Students to Plan and Organize Research

The words of warning that Jesus gives about counting the cost before attempting projects are clear.

> Suppose one of you wants to build a tower. Won't you first sit down and estimate the cost to see if you have enough money to complete it? For if you lay the foundation and are not able to finish it, everyone who sees it will ridicule you, saying, 'This person began to build and wasn't able to finish.' (Luke 14:28–30)

While the focus of this saying of Jesus is on counting the cost of being a disciple, the principle clearly has wider application. The length of the doctorate varies. In some contexts it is three or four years, but where there is a coursework component, this can mean it takes five or six years to complete. Spending up to six years is a large portion of a student's life and ministry to invest in doing a doctorate. They need to be absolutely sure that this is the right thing for them to do, and that they can undertake it wholeheartedly, and without regrets.

So too is the large investment of money needed by the student and their supporters to gain a doctoral qualification. The student should be sure whether this is the most strategic way for those funds to be invested for the future. Moreover, is there a clear financial pathway through, or will the project run into difficulties through lack of funding?

Time: Planning and Management

This section focuses on the thesis / dissertation-writing component of doctoral study. For doctoral programs with coursework, there is more structure and accountability with regular classes, seminars, and formal assessments in the first years. Many students find, in moving from the early stage of such a course, or a taught postgraduate masters degree, that the freedom and lack of structure in the thesis / dissertation-writing stage can be a challenge and a problem. Some thrive on the autonomy. Many don't. This is why previous experience of preparing other exercises of independent learning / research is very important.

Supervisors need to help scholars to manage this learning process. They need an appropriate structure and strategies to work with through the duration of this period of study. Part of this strategy must be that the individual takes more ownership for managing their own learning as the project develops.

This means enabling the student to gradually take control of the project which they bring to completion. These are vital skills for the 'self-managing learner' for a future ministry of teaching, research, and writing.

Some students react against planning, and prefer to 'see how it goes', and to 'muddle through' somehow. While there is a need for flexibility, and continuous review and revision of timelines, generally people work best to deadlines. The old saying that 'if you aim at nothing, you are bound to hit it' is very apposite.

Doing the Calculations

Here's the chance for a quick mathematics lesson. It is a useful exercise to work through this with a student at one of the first supervisory sessions.

Working on the number of years available in the doctoral program for thesis / dissertation writing (adjust the time pro-rata according to the time expected for a student to write their thesis in your doctoral program – usually two to four years) – how many days do they have to write a doctoral thesis?[1]

If the thesis-writing stage is three years, over a thousand days seems a long time. Time to go in a slow and relaxed manner, plenty of time to take it easy, and make leisurely research trips. Well, instead, time passes remarkably quickly, and before long it doesn't seem like half long enough. But students won't be working all day every day.

Starting with the total number of days for the writing, some deductions will now need to be made.

Will the student work at weekends?

> It is important that students maintain good relationships with a local church, and maybe do some preaching or other ministry from time to time. Assume they will not work on Sundays, so deduct the total number of Sundays there are over the years of thesis writing from your initial total.

Family time:

> The student may have a family, and one of the problems doctoral students face is neglect of family during intense periods of study. So allow for a certain

---

1. Assuming no leap years, your answer should be 1095 days!

number of family days (usually on Saturdays when children are off school) across the years of thesis writing, and deduct them from the total.

Rest and recreation:

Students also need 'down-time' – opportunity for rest and recreation from time to time. They are likely to want a holiday. So deduct the number of days for annual holidays over the years available for thesis / dissertation writing. Also deduct the days for 'statutory holidays' – Christmas, New Year, National Holidays and Festivals when libraries may be closed.

Illness or accident:

It is also quite likely that over the years of thesis writing there will be time when the student, or someone in their family, will be ill. There may even, sadly, be time when a close relative dies and there is need to return home for a funeral. So deduct an allowance for illness or accidents.

Family events:

There will need to be time for key family events – children's birthdays, weddings, anniversaries, school sports days, etc. Deduct a figure from your total for this.

Teaching and tutoring:

Also within the doctoral program, there may be a provision to act as a Teaching Assistant or Research Assistant, or to prepare and deliver some seminars, so deduct a figure for the number of days that will be given to that.

Your calculation should look something like this:

Total number of days in [2, 3, 4] years   =_____
Minus
- Sundays (over years of dissertation writing)   =
- Holidays (over years of dissertation writing)   =
- Illness or accident (over years of dissertation writing)   =
- Family events (over years of dissertation writing)   =
- Teaching Assistant role or seminar preparation   =
Final total   =_____

You will probably find that if the thesis is written over three years, the total is now more like 700 days than 1,095 days.

Planning Styles

At an early stage of the thesis supervision, the supervisor should discuss planning and work styles with a student. Get the student to articulate how they have planned previous major pieces of work in the past. Discuss plans they have to research and write articles, make presentations, and produce chapters in their thesis.

- Not all doctoral projects develop, or can be developed in a linear, sequential fashion. This needs to be discussed at an early stage with the student, so they need to be prepared to do some things out of sequence. Discuss the parts of the plan where this is likely to occur, e.g. fieldwork or archival research.
- Some students find it easier to plan by depicting their thesis, or section of work, using the mind-mapping approach – creating a structure through a series of interconnected 'thought bubbles' – which revolve around a central concept. The result is a complex diagram with a series of related tasks and sub-tasks, and arrows between them.[2] These then need to be ordered into a logical structure.
- Although the result is not a linear line of tasks, a process with timelines still needs to be developed arising from this.

Discuss a range of planning styles with your students:
- For major pieces of work
- For small essays, articles or chapters

Dividing Up the Time Allowed

But time-planning should not stop there.

Now get the student to allocate the total time available across the key tasks in writing a thesis. The model below is based on the three-year full-time model, but this can be allocated on a pro-rata basis. In some doctoral programs with a coursework phase some of these tasks are done before the thesis-writing stage starts.

---

2. E.g. A. Buzan, *The Mind Map* (London: BBC Active, 2009), and see other titles by Buzan. The approach is reviewed in J. C. Nesbit and O. O. Adesope, 'Learning with Concept and Knowledge Maps: A Aeta-Analysis,' *Review of Educational Research* 76, no. 3 (2006): 413.

Year 1

How many days of the total available do you allocate to:

i)   Clarifying the topic for research, identifying an original problem?

DAYS ALLOCATED =

This is a key area to develop at an early stage. In some fields the topic is clear, in others you are not sure where the material will take you, and how the field will open up. This means that there are elements over which you don't have control, and a certain amount of flexibility is needed.

ii) Identifying and accessing appropriate library or archive-based materials.

DAYS ALLOCATED =

This is important and may require a pilot study and research visits if the materials are not held in local libraries.

iii) Identifying areas where fieldwork research is needed, where this will be done, how it is to be done, and its scope.

DAYS ALLOCATED =

iv) Setting research in the context of previous knowledge and current studies.

DAYS ALLOCATED =

The focus here is on the literature review, which is more controllable than other aspects. This helps define the scope of the project. In some fields the scholarly literature is vast, and needs to be managed so it is achievable in the time allowed.

v)   Undertaking necessary training in research methods and skills; language study (if needed).

DAYS ALLOCATED =

vi) Beginning collection of information and / or investigations using appropriate methodologies.

DAYS ALLOCATED =

vii) Writing initial draft chapter(s).

DAYS ALLOCATED =

It is important to get students writing early and regularly, when ideas are fresh in their minds. Each research task should include some writing component. Writing is a skill that is learned over time, and with experience.

viii) Preparing for annual review / upgrade.

DAYS ALLOCATED =

Reporting is a vital skill to learn, and needs to be seen as an important reflective tool rather than an onerous chore. It allows assessment of what has been achieved, and how it has been done, but feeds into review of the state of the project, and allows for planning for the next phases.

It also allows students to step back and reflect in the broader sense on what they have achieved and will do.

This is a good point at which to discuss which potential research leads are followed in the next year, and which ones are to be given up.

The review allows for setting out conclusions so far, and recommendations, for discussion and assessment. It also allows for communication of findings, and so reviews should be robust and be a form of preparation for final oral examination. Most reviews ask for a timeline for the envisaged completion of the thesis, which is a further planning tool.

Keeping Good Records Is Vital

Projects evolve and change, and the need to recognize and chart those changes is important. A Research Journal is a good way to record this process of development.

Year 2

The project should now be well established, with a structure emerging, and a likely time for completion developing.

How many days do you allocate to . . .?

 i)   collection and recording of information and / or investigations using appropriate methodologies (this may include a significant fieldwork component) _____

 ii)   analysing findings / information _____

 iii)   placing findings alongside those of others _____

iv) developing theoretical concepts (thinking) _____

v) writing further draft chapters (up to half of the full draft of chapters required) _____

vi) attending a key conference? _____
- This is an important dimension of developing research skills, allowing access to the wider academic discourse in the field. It is essential for developing the work, and making key contacts with dialogue partners and academic peers.

vii) preparing for annual review / upgrade _____
- Upgrade meetings are especially helpful if they include a presentation. They make the student focus on finding ways of expressing what the key research idea is, why the research is important, what the key questions / hypotheses are, what tasks are needed. It is important that supervisors spend some time working through these issues and possible presentations with the student in advance of the meeting.

Year 3

First Six Months
How many days should be allocated to . . .?

i) completing collection of information and / or investigations using appropriate methodologies _____

ii) completing recording, managing of information and findings _____

iii) critically evaluating findings and those of others, and developing theoretical concepts, developing originality and independent thinking _____

iv) integrating findings with those of others in secondary literature _____

v) completing draft chapters _____

vi) presenting seminar / conference paper_____
- At this stage a paper will be of ideas that have become clearer and taken more of a fixed form – as a thesis is emerging. The presentation gives an opportunity for testing out hypotheses, gauging the state of academic discourse.

Second Six Months

How much time should be allocated to . . .?

 i)   producing a fully revised final draft of thesis _____

 ii) writing the introduction and conclusions _____

 iii) ensuring the thesis has coherence and originality_____

 iv) creating Bibliography, correctly producing references, ensuring high-level proof reading _____

 v)   final presentation of research outcomes in a thesis _____

 vi) submitting notice of intention of submission _____

 vii) presenting and defending the outcomes of research in examination _____

 viii) making any revisions requested by examiners _____

The Value of Planning

Without letting it become unduly restrictive or limiting of the flow of academic ideas and creative approaches, time spent by the supervisor in supporting the student with their planning gives an accountability structure to the process.

In supervision, it is good to have meetings devoted to assessing progress so far, and the plan for completion of the thesis. This can be done a couple of times a year, rather than just focusing on a piece of work.

It is important that the supervisor ensures that reviewing and planning are not put off by the student. These key review meetings can be charted on to an annual year planner by the student and supervisor – and the key outcomes marked out.

Charting the Major Milestones of Thesis Writing

One question doctoral students often ask is, 'am I on track', 'will I be finished in time'. It is good to have in mind a rough time chart.

There is a final time limit on when the thesis needs to be completed, which is the ultimate deadline. Working back from that point in planning creates a series of deadlines that become staging posts along the route, and allow progress to be calibrated and celebrated.

According to your understanding of the process, set out what you think should have been achieved at different points (adjust according to the timescale in your own doctoral program).

After 3 months the student should have . . .

After 6 months the student should have . . .

After 1 year the student should have . . .

After 18 months the student should have . . .

After 2 years the student should have . . .

After 30 months the student will have . . .

After 3 years the student must have . . .

Breaking the Task Down

When accomplishing a major, or arduous, undertaking, such as climbing a mountain, or taking a long journey, it is best to break it down into a series of smaller, more manageable tasks. This makes the project seem less overwhelming.

Supervisors should help students to break the key stages into a series of tasks that can be accomplished within monthly timeframes. This means that each period is accounted for. Students should be personally encouraged to start each week afresh with a planning hour. This should be a matter for prayer, and committed to God. Progress can be reviewed at the end of the week.

Students should develop a list of measurable outcomes at regular intervals. When students can see exactly when they are expected to do key tasks, it gives structure to the process. Students need to rank tasks as high and low priority. These can be recorded in a research journal.

Sometimes students feel that time is passing, and they have not achieved very much. The planning process and a time chart allows them the opportunity to review what has been achieved and gain a sense of progress being made.

Missed Targets

If targets are regularly missed, what does it show?

i) Does the student need to work harder and faster?

ii) Does the student need to allot more time to tasks, and be more realistic in planning?

iii) Is there a need to scale down objectives, attempt less, make the project smaller or more focused?

iv) Do some aspects of the project need to be abandoned?

The student may find that the work is done more quickly than envisaged. If that is the case, are there extra dimensions that need to be added to broaden the project out?

The Limitations of Planning

Planning should be a tool that brings focus and direction, and a sense of achievement when targets are met. It is notoriously difficult to predict how doctoral theses will turn out, and when they will be completed. Usually, tasks take longer than we expect. Deadlines will shift about, and there should not be excessive anxiety about that, as long as an eye is kept on the ticking clock.

Celebrating Planning

i)   It reduces the risk of overlooking something important

ii)   It helps the student realize when they have hit problems and not met planned targets

iii) It helps students see relationships between activities

iv)   It renders activities into a manageable order

v)   It helps keep track of resources you can control, and identify others you need

vi)   Planning indicates what is feasible

vii) It helps to identify training needs

viii) Planning provides discipline and motivation as targets are set and met. It turns the big mountain to be climbed into a series of smaller climbs of manageable proportions.

ix)   People do work better to deadlines.

In all this the supervisor has an important role. They can see issues and celebrate achievements in a way that students in the maelstrom of their studies and thoughts often cannot. Also, the experienced supervisor will have led students through the process before, can chart the path to the end, and direct the student towards it.

Handling Problems

There are times in the doctoral process when major problems emerge. Perhaps the student's ideas don't work out. Their working hypothesis does not appear to be holding true, or there is not the material they expected to find. When this happens, the use of a planning meeting is valuable to decide what to do. In the meeting, ask the student to write the problem down, and identify exactly what the issues are. Then discuss the solutions that are available.

At other times the student may have encountered a period of illness, or family crisis, and lost time. Again, this is the time to meet, and assess the options available. Is some form of suspension of studies needed, or leave of absence? What sort of medical or pastoral certification will be needed for that?

The supervisor should not let the student leave a crisis unresolved or unaddressed.

Financial Planning

While this is not a direct area of the supervisor's responsibility, and the supervisor will do well not to be drawn into the details of a student's financial situation, there will be times when the supervisor is aware of the problems that the student is facing in the area of finance. This is a very common reason for students to slow the pace of their studies, or need to take a break from them, and the warning signs need to be spotted early.

It is important that when a student is considering a research degree that they have an adequate financial plan. Part of the application process, and the student induction, should be for a finance officer to walk the student through the potential financial challenges when considering research.

On the next page there is a sample outline that can be used on these occasions, so that, as in the parable of Jesus, the 'cost can be counted'.

THE TOTAL COST OF DOING A DOCTORATE

Tuition Fees

Other Amenity Fees (e.g. library, student facilities, etc.) _____

Accomodation Costs _____

Personal Living Costs (e.g. food, heat, light, telephone, Internet, etc.) _____

Medical and Personal Insurances _____

Dependants' Maintenance _____

Dependants' Medical Costs, Insurance, School Fees _____

Cost of Travel (to place of study) _____

Cost of Relocation to Institution of Study (if necessary), or Travel
to Visit Family

Personal Study Resources (e.g. laptop, software, repairs, paper,
pens, etc.) _____

Books, scanning, photocopying _____

Loss of Incomes _____

Interest on Loans _____

Cost of Research and External Library Visits _____

Conference Attendance and Travel _____

Other Costs _____

Contingencies _____

TOTAL EXPECTED COSTS ═══════════

Against this should be set

Expected Earned Income _____

Bursaries / Scholarships / Grants _____

Donations (e.g. from family, church, etc.) _____

Mission Agency Support _____

Loans (e.g. student loans or loans from family members) _____

TOTAL EXPECTED INCOME ═══════════

Do the student's resources match the opportunity?

Further Reading

Murray, R. *How to Write a Thesis*, 2nd edition. Maidenhead: Open University Press, 2006.

Phillips, E. M., and D. S. Pugh. *How to Get a PhD: A Handbook for Students and Their Supervisors*. Maidenhead: Open University Press, 2010 (Kindle edition available also.)

7

Getting Research Students Started

Providing doctoral students with appropriate academic advice and support at the beginning and throughout the duration of their programs is vital equipment for success in doctoral programs.[1]

One of the important issues in starting the supervisory process is establishing the parameters for supervision at one of the first supervisory meetings. This will be discussed in chapter 9 of this handbook. As well as establishing that pattern, the first few months of a doctoral research project are crucial in other ways. There are aspects in which the student needs to 'upskill', but this can take time, and there is a danger in this process that time can drift, and little progress made. That can be discouraging to the student. There is a need to combine gaining the necessary induction and training, with some writing projects that move the research forward.

Induction

Induction is important because it sets the student up for the rest of the educational experience. Students need to understand thoroughly the program upon which they have embarked, and the resources available to them, and the induction program helps them to do this.

Each doctoral program should begin with an induction process for all new students. This usually takes the form of a course run in the first few weeks of the program, reflecting the specific needs of doctoral students and providing appropriate information about the institution, its programs, codes of conduct, student responsibilities, facilities available, health and safety issues. Key information should also be presented in the form of a doctoral handbook / calendar. It is not sufficient simply to give the student the handbook

---

1. Shaw, *Best Practice*, Section 15.

and ask them to read it, because most won't! Instead, its context needs to be explained and opportunity to ask questions given. It is also the responsibility of the supervisor to know its contents in detail, so you will need to read it too!

After initial induction other research training opportunities should be provided at regular intervals throughout the duration of the doctoral program, in order to progressively build research and professional skills. Induction leads into training, which is a continuous process.

The ICETE *Best Practice Guidelines* set out the aspects of Research Induction that should be made available to the doctoral student.[2] Although much of this will be delivered institutionally, or even by facilitators external to the institution, it is the responsibility of the research supervisor to ensure that the student is able to benefit from what is available.

This research skills training should cover topics such as:

i) Understanding how learning happens at doctoral level.

ii) Research methodology, and developing skills in epistemology, and meta-level reflection.

iii) Building analytical and synthetic skills; framing research questions.

iv) Written communication skills for the academic context, and for beyond the academic context.

v) Research ethics, and approaches to human-subject research. This is very important, and institutional policies on this need to be clear. Appropriate safeguards, permissions and consents for use of materials, and issues relating to confidentiality of sensitive materials all need to be clearly understood and acted on.

vi) The Christian understanding of research and doctoral education, including the role of research within the *missio Dei*.

vii) Oral presentation and discourse skills:
- Giving research papers.
- Discussing the research findings of others.

viii) Computing skills and accessing electronic resources.

ix) Bibliographic skills.

x) Use of electronic resources and web-based materials.

---

2. Ibid.

xi)   Project planning and time management.

xii) Record keeping and record management.

Other skills for professional development and leadership in theological education also need to be taught, and these are usually delivered through training events delivered at regular intervals during a student's doctoral program.

These include:

i)   Approaches to participation in seminars, workshops and academic conferences.

ii)   Preparation for examination.

iii) Personal and career development, and future employment planning.

iv)   Utilizing the doctoral qualification after it has been completed. This should include:
- Teaching and lecturing skills (pedagogy, andragogy).
- Academic administration.
- Life after the doctorate – ongoing research, writing, integrating ongoing research into service for the Kingdom of God.
- Scholarship as lifelong vocation.
- Theological education and mission.
- Writing for publication.

Recording and Storage of Research Material

It is important to talk through with students the best ways of organizing their research findings so they can be easily accessed. This may be covered in general in the overall research induction process, but make sure the students have applied the material specifically to their situation and subject area.
- Smooth and efficient methods of data storage and retrieval are essential.
- Ways of arranging notes and systems of cross-referencing need to be discussed.
- How will the student store materials they gather? Whether written notes, scans, or photocopies, how will they ensure they can find what they are looking for?
- What index system will they use?
- It is important to establish at the outset which writing style guide (such as the *Chicago Manual for Writers of Theses*) will be used in writing the project. This ensures that all references are stored in the correct form from the beginning of research, to save hours of checking references later.
- A Research Journal is a helpful way of recording what research activities were undertaken and where the results are stored.

Security of Research Findings Is All Important

The mantra is clear – backup, backup, and backup again!

I can give examples of students who have had laptops stolen containing all their research work and writing – and in one case they gave up and never completed their doctorate. When I was nearing the completion of my thesis I had a copy stored on the hard disk of my computer, and another separately on old floppy disks (yes it was a long time ago!). I also had a paper copy of the drafts of chapters stored at my parent's house fifty miles away. There was no way I could face having to re-research and rewrite the whole thesis if there was a fire or robbery at my home! Nowadays the use of the 'cloud' for secure, accessible, off-site storage is recommended, provided the student can maintain any subscription required.

Specific Research Induction to the Field

As well as more general introduction to research methodologies, more specific induction will be needed into the candidate's field. Sometimes students are frustrated that there is not more detailed induction in their subject area, and it will fall to the supervisor to provide that where needed. Specific research skills and methods will need to be developed or reinforced.

This is often a key area that supervisors don't see as important, or forget about – and it creates problems for scholars.

Here is a useful series of steps:

Initial Training

Conduct an initial training needs analysis. This should be done at an early stage, and covers issues such as:

i)   What skills does the student already have?

ii)   What further skills does the student need? (e.g. data gathering, management, record keeping, IT skills, communication skills)

iii) Especially in biblical subjects, but also in other theological and historical fields, they may need other languages – German, French, Latin – as well as enhanced Hebrew / Greek.

iv)   The supervisor needs to know what opportunities and resources there are to assist with language learning. Are there specific courses?

v)   At what point in the student's course is the language learning best done, so they are equipped when the skills are needed?

vi)   Are there further postgraduate courses, workshops, training programs available in the seminary / university that students will benefit from?

vii)   Supervisors need to be aware of what is available and what will be beneficial. You should not just rely on the student being able to find these themselves.

viii)   Is funding available for these extra training needs?

ix)   At what point in the program will the extra training be needed? This needs to be agreed with the supervisor, and fitted into the research plan.

x)   Training needs should be evaluated at least annually – as the project develops, or changes, research needs may change.

Reflective Questions

What specific research skills did you need for your doctorate?

How did you access those skills?

What are the needs of your current PhD student?

Of the research skills the student needs, which can you provide, and which will need to be provided from elsewhere?

Key Attainment Goals for Students in the First Months of Supervision

i)   The research problem needs to be stated clearly.

ii)   Research design needs to be clear and the research proposal revised, and if it has not already been approved, it should be now.

iii)   The methods for data collection and storage need to be established.

iv)   The research ethics issues related to the project need to be understood and agreed.

v)   Proper access to library resources in the institution or elsewhere needs to be negotiated.

vi)   A pilot study might be needed.

Starting Students Writing

Students need to develop their writing skills quickly. This is vital not only for their thesis, but for other aspects of their doctoral-level work, including preparing reports, seminar papers, conference presentations and academic papers.

It is important at an early stage for students to begin to get their ideas and research findings on paper, so that they can later develop these further. This means moving students into writing mode as soon as possible. Although students will already have experience of different forms of writing, it is still good for them to write short pieces at what will become doctoral-level work.

From the outset, the supervisor should require the student to show high levels of spelling, grammar, editing, and referencing, in order to establish skills and expectations. Putting this work in early, and gaining practice of exercising these skills, makes editing the final version a simpler, and less lengthy process.

Supervisors have different policies on correcting the language and grammar of their students, but it is recognized that the academic strength of a piece of work is less easy to appreciate when the text is littered with spelling or grammatical errors, or the sense is not comprehensible. Where a student is not writing in their first language they should get assistance with their style and expression from an experienced proofreader. It must be made clear that this support does not involve 'help' or 'correcting' issues of content or argument.

As well as developing skills in written prose, students also need to continue to apply those of planning sections of text, and producing workable outlines. They need to develop ways of constructing chapter titles and introductions that mean they get the best out of their material.

They also need to develop skills in reviewing their own writing to see what is good and bad.

Reflective Questions

What do you think will be added to the scholar's research by reviewing the 'state of the art' scholarship in their subject area?

What are the strengths of doing this at the start of the research project, and what are the strengths of doing this towards the end?

Reviewing Literature

One helpful approach to getting students writing quickly is to ask them to produce short reviews (200–500 words) of key texts in their subject area. These pieces can build together into the literature review, so the student feels their initial work is already contributing to the thesis.

Locating Sources

In the initial stages, supervisors need to point students in the direction of sources they need to read to develop their research. Here are some starting points:

i)   The key texts by leading scholars should contain extensive bibliographies of published and unpublished material.

ii) Academic journals contain articles, and also book reviews. Some produce an annual listing of books, articles, and theses in specific subject areas.

iii) Library catalogues are an essential source, and many are available online now, including major holding libraries such as the Library of Congress and the British Library.

iv) Online search engines host many databases of academic journals and will yield the best of recent resources.

v)   Databases of recently published theses should be consulted by doctoral students – it is essential to be aware of the latest research.

vi) Personal contacts and dialogue with other scholars. This may take place at conferences, or through personal correspondence, etc.

Research Needs to Be Set in the Context of Wider Scholarship

The 'Literature' to be reviewed is scholarly contributions from the research field – including books, journal articles, conference and seminar papers (some unpublished), ejournals, academic websites, online debates and reports of conferences.

Academic journals and conference papers usually contain material at the cutting edge of research, and it is crucial that doctoral students consult these. This is often where scholars think aloud, and present their research findings for review for the first time, with a view to receiving initial feedback from their academic peers.

One thing helpful for students is to read reviews of key texts in journals done by other scholars. This will allow them to see approaches established scholars have taken, and the strengths and weaknesses they have identified. Students can be encouraged to critique these reviews. However, this is no substitute for reading the work themselves, and forming their own critical evaluation.

The Purpose of the Literature Review in the Thesis

An examiner of a doctoral thesis will want to know if the student has:

i)   Extensive knowledge of the subject.

ii)   Made a critical review of other academic material core to the field. The student needs to demonstrate that they know exactly where the field is in terms of current scholarship. The doctoral thesis should be capable in some way of changing the field.

iii) Good awareness of how their research is different from other scholarship and does not replicate it.

iv)   Kept on reading from the time when the thesis has started. The field can significantly change in the three or four years (or more) it may take to write a thesis. If the literature review was undertaken three years previously and not updated, it may contain significant gaps.

v)   Kept on reading between the submission and examination to be aware of other research being published or theses being presented.

vi)   Demonstrated the relationship between their work and that in the rest of the field, so that they can make connections between their own research findings, and the 'state of the art' scholarship.

Forms of Literature Reviews

i)   An initial survey of the important material in the field.

This produces a list of the 'must read' texts in the field. In its initial form this will appear in the research proposal.

ii)   A summary of the current knowledge base, and analysis of the types of investigation others have used in the field.

This comprehensive review will demonstrate an understanding of the main schools of thought, and will establish the extent of current research, especially that done recently. The well-worked areas of the field will emerge, together with the areas where there are significant gaps. The supervisor can encourage the student to develop research in these directions so that it serves as an 'original contribution to knowledge'.

This dimension of the literature review establishes the key research questions that need to be posed, or tested, and is best done at an early stage of the research.

iii)   Review of methodologies

The literature review also establishes the main methodologies in the field, and the way different academic positions have emerged. Again, the value in doing this work early in the research process is evident. It will help the student identify and establish the approach they will take, and show an awareness of its strengths and weaknesses.

iv)   Establishing the boundaries

The literature review is where the student is able to delimit the field they are tackling. In it the student can set the boundaries, and define what will be covered.

Literature Reviews Also Serve a Number of Other Purposes

- Creating Dialogue Partners

   This is essential to participating in academic discourse. The writings of other scholars become dialogue partners, providing material to develop, endorse, challenge, or revise.

- A Level Check

   The scholarly literature that doctoral students engage with allows them to check not only what others are saying about their subject, but also the level at which they are writing. At first students may feel they can never attain that level, but as they gain in confidence, they start to identify ways in which they are writing at the level of their academic peers.

   As they progress in their course doctoral students should be able to critique effectively the work of others. Eventually they should be able to say, if this scholar's work was presented as a doctoral thesis, would it pass?

   If not, why not?

- 'Are they thinking what I am thinking?'

   The writings of other scholars become a 'sounding board', against which the scholar's own views are tested.

Does what the scholar is saying stand up to the scrutiny of other scholars? Are they thinking in the way that the scholar is thinking? If not, why not? Are the ideas the scholar proposes brilliant and original, or untenable, or even crazy!

This makes the literature review take the form of a safety check, allowing comparison of ideas and levels.

- 'This is important'

    Through extensive dialogue with the literature in their field, the student is able to see the necessity and legitimacy of their study, and to make a clear argument for its importance. The student's research should emerge from the survey of the field, and 'mesh' with it at appropriate points. The literature review does more than merely set the scene. Throughout the rest of the thesis the student needs to refer back to the key literature, and maintain a dialogue with it. One of the dangers of many literature reviews is that they remain hermetically sealed chapters, which bear little relationship to the other sections of the thesis, rather than being a central part of the flow of narrative and logic.

The Literature Review Needs to Be Constantly Updated

Scholarship is changing – students must feed new material into their developing draft at appropriate points.

Scope of the Literature Review

One issue that frequently arises is the question of how much, or how little, material constitutes an adequate literature review.

The project the student is undertaking may be groundbreaking, and there may be little secondary literature within the precise field. However, that should not prevent a review being undertaken. There will be literature in related and integrated fields where the material is relevant, and forms a context for the work. There will also be a range of sources that can be explored which allow comparative study to be undertaken.

If the scope of the secondary literature in the student's field is too vast to be reviewed, it may mean that the project is too broad, and needs to be narrowed.

Reflective Questions

How would you advise a student when they report that there is little secondary material in their chosen field?

What parallel topics, or methodological approaches can be considered?

The Supervisor's Responsibilities

All this places a significant responsibility on the supervisor.

Supervisors need to know the research field well. They need to know the secondary literature thoroughly so that gaps in the student's work can be identified. It is important not to supervise students outside your own research field or area of competence, to ensure students are not disadvantaged by gaps in your knowledge. Where a project contains elements significantly outside the research field of a supervisor, either the supervisory team needs to be strengthened by members who have that expertise, or the project given to another supervisor who has the specific knowledge needed.

It is an essential requirement of supervisors that they are research and writing active, so that they themselves are at the cutting edge of the field.

It is not possible to give students an adequate supervisory experience solely based on knowledge and research experience gained doing your own PhD ten or fifteen years ago.

Further Reading

Murray, R. *How to Write a Thesis*. Maidenhead: Open University, 2002.

Phillips, E. M., and D. S. Pugh. *How to Get a PhD: A Handbook for Students and Their Supervisors*. Maidenhead: Open University Press, 2010. (Kindle edition available also.)

Potter, S. *Doing Postgraduate Research*. London: Sage, 2006.

Smith, K. *Writing and Research: A Guide for Theological Students*. Carlisle: Langham Global Library, 2015

Taylor, Stan, and Nigel Beasley. *A Handbook for Doctoral Supervisors*. New York: Routledge, 2005.

8

Framing Research Questions and the Research Proposal

'In order to succeed we must learn to ask the right questions' – Aristotle

At the heart of critical thinking (reflective judgment) is the ability to ask questions. Not just any questions, but the right ones. We question in order to gain knowledge and understanding.

My son and I were recently working on an old tractor engine that had stood unused for many years. We reached a point in working on the carburettor where we could not see how one part of it fitted back together. Who could we ask? My father would have known, but sadly he is no longer alive. So my son found the part number, the model, and make and Googled it. And, amazingly, there was a Youtube video of some old guy in his back yard dismantling and putting back together the same ancient carburettor we had before us. Problem solved. The solution was in the 'crowd knowledge' that the Internet opens up.

But that solution was only possible by putting in the right details and asking the right questions.

Doctoral Students need to be trained in how to ask the right questions. This is because developing specific research questions,

- enables us to understand the Other (i.e. that which is not yet known).
- helps us to deploy our God-given rationality and capacity for critical reflection.
- opens up an exciting hermeneutical journey.

Reflective Questions

Think back to your own PhD study.

What were the three most key questions you needed to ask?

How did you go about identifying those questions?

There is a close connection between being a good researcher and knowing how to ask the right questions. As we have already seen, the image of the lawyer in court is helpful. The ability to probe, question, take unusual angles, dig beneath the surface in cross-examination, often yields the truth which may be being concealed. Similarly, the doctoral student needs to be a good critical thinker, and to be able to demonstrate purposeful and reflective judgment about what to believe or what to do in response to observations, experience, verbal or written expressions, or arguments.

The critical thinker needs to use not only logic, to also be able to effectively demonstrate intellectual abilities such as accuracy, relevance, analysis and synthesis, and academic balance.

In demonstrating these abilities, devising the correct series of questions is vital.

The Community Dimension

The process of formulating questions can be difficult to the lone researcher. They sometimes arise more naturally through discussion and dialogue. Articulating the issues in debate, and explaining them to others, often helps students to 'see' issues much more clearly.

As a supervisor, being an informed dialogue partner is of vital assistance to the student. It enables:

- A fusion of horizons – the supervisor's perspectives are used to refine or enhance those of the student.
- Dialogical reflection. I can recall many cases where a research student I have supervised gets apparently stuck at a certain point of their thinking, and is not making progress. But through 'talking the issue out' clarity is brought. It does not necessarily mean the supervisor telling the student what the solution is – it is a much better learning experience for the student to come to see that for himself / herself. However, sometimes direction in this is needed.
- Dialogue with those in other subject areas, which can also raise profound questions and bring new insights.

Those Big Questions

Sometimes the biggest questions come in the shortest form – especially those core ones. Why, what, how?

I have a little cartoon that I sometimes show my students to illustrate this. It is of a boy going up to his father, and saying 'Dad, you know how I am always asking questions . . . Why?'

The Why? question paves the way for analysis and evaluation of facts, ideas and events. It probes into the reasons behind an issue.

The What? question opens up a way to outlining and describing the nature of the subject field, and the issues it raises. It helps to both open up, and delimit, the research and the hypotheses to be explored.

The How? question opens up exploration of how something works, how it has come together, how it is organized or appears. It leads into methodological issues – the way one interprets the data. Using the right method will help yield the most helpful results.

Persistence

Doctoral students need to be dogged and relentless in their ability to raise questions, and pursue them, setting aside simplistic answers by probing ever more deeply. In supervision sessions, especially at the early stages of a doctoral project, it is important to get students to clarify what questions their research is designed to provide answers for. The supervisor therefore needs to be relentless in her / his own questioning of the student – on what basis did you make that argument? Why did it come at that point in the chapter? Why have you chosen this approach? How did you come to the conclusion? Where does this lead? These are the 'iron sharpening iron' questions, designed to make the student think, and then think again more deeply. They will need to articulate their reasons in the thesis and to their examiners, so it is good for students to have experience of doing that verbally in the early stages of their work.

Questioning Texts

Critical thinkers need to read texts closely, and then write effectively about them.

As they read key texts and primary source material, they must interrogate them with a series of questions. These must be,

- vital questions and formulated clearly and precisely;
- designed to collect relevant information;
- created to help students use theoretical constructs from the wider field to bring effective interpretations;
- able to yield conclusions and solutions that can be tested;
- designed to allow the student to remain open minded about alternative solutions;
- capable of yielding findings, and solutions that are effectively communicated;
- a means to building new or alternative hypotheses, or challenging existing ones.

In doing this, the student is effectively bringing other scholars or their writings into the courtroom, and cross-examining them so that they provide in-depth answers.

Research is 'RE' + Search – often going over ideas and paths that others have trodden, but with new eyes, using new and improved techniques, and making connections that have not been made before.

It is surprising how much secondary literature is based on summaries of other secondary literature, without the original sources being read. In a thesis the student must demonstrate first-hand familiarity with the writings of the most important advocates in their field, and give evidence that they have critically interacted with them. Examiners may well demand parts of the thesis be rewritten in places where primary sources have not been used and the thesis is dependent on secondary sources.

A Summary of the Process

Asking the right questions (critical thinking)
>   of the right sources
>>   in the right way (methodology)
>>>   in order to gather information
>>>>   that can be interpreted and recorded with fresh insight
>>>>>   leading toward creative recommendations and actions
>>>>>>   according to God's will and for his glory. (cf. Phil 1:9–11)

Exercise

Give a list of what core skills you think are needed to develop the right research questions.

Ways of Developing the Key Questions

Students must learn to:

- Listen to the current state of scholarship.
- Listen to their sources – their voice needs to be heard, and respected, and not read through other interpreters who may have got it wrong.
- Listen to God – research is an aspect of glorifying God with our minds, so he needs to be included in the process. Prayer can move mountains, and help move obstacles in the way of the researcher.

At an initial stage students should work with the supervisor to:

1)   Look for a key question that breaks down into a series of supplementary questions

2)   Reflect on the questions they have proposed:

    i)   Do the questions go deep enough?

    ii)   Are they capable of opening up the research field? If not, are they too narrow?

    iii)   Are they capable of being answered? If not, are they too wide?

    iv)   Which of these key questions are the ones that can be used as the focus for the thesis / dissertation?

Checks and Balances: Problems to Avoid

1. 'I already know the answers.'
This yields 'closed' research. The student has decided what the result of the research will be before it has been undertaken. In the light of this, it is likely that there will not be an objective assessment of evidence, for the student's mind is made up. Sources will tend to be read in the way that supports their theory.

2. 'God will provide me with the answers.'
This is a hyper-spiritual approach. Martin Luther lamented those Christians who had a view of God's providence such that they believed that if they were hungry they simply needed to open their mouth and a roasted chicken would fly into it! As Christian teachers, we do believe that God can and does provide answers. But he normally does that through means, which are the proper use of God-given rationality, hard study, gathering evidence, and careful analysis of it. You need to do more than just open your mouth!

3. The research won't make any difference.
This suggests a lack of motivation in undertaking the project. To spend three to five years on a research doctorate needs drive and purpose. If the topic seems irrelevant to current or future needs, students may become demotivated and disinterested.

Here are key motivators in research to encourage Christian students you are supervising:
- this is done for the honor and glory of God;
- this will develop students as servants of Christ;
- the students who subject themselves to this hard work and detailed process will deepen their minds;
- this will enable students to contribute to the mission of God by allowing their voices to be heard in the academic field;
- this will build research and other skills for future work.

Reflective Questions

How can you as a doctoral supervisor help your doctoral students most in developing their research questions?

RIGHT AND WRONG QUESTIONS

1 Chronicles 21:1–17 gives an example of a research project that was certainly very interesting, but displeased God.

What was wrong in David's motivations?

What might David have thought he could achieve by this research?

How can supervisors help students to avoid working on unhelpful or unfruitful topics?

The Research Proposal

As we have seen in a previous chapter, critical thinking is the exercise of purposeful and reflective judgment about complex issues. It involves deciding what we should we do in response to observations, experience, verbal or written expressions, or arguments that we encounter. Critical thinking demands asking questions with clarity, accuracy, relevance, depth, breadth, significance and fairness.

The place for the development of the questions that drive the research project is in the research proposal. This is a major exercise which is undertaken before the thesis research starts properly. When written, it should be a piece of significant length, and include a well-developed indicative bibliography.

For many students this can be a crisis point, and take much longer than expected. For those who have not written a significant piece of independent research at masters level, or are from educational contexts where critical reflection is not encouraged, it is especially difficult.

The skills of the student are still at an early stage, and supervisors need to strike a careful balance between leaving students floundering in uncertainty and lack of direction, and being over-directive and effectively writing the proposal for the student. It is, after all, the student's project.

Here is an example of a research proposal outline that some have found helpful, and could be used to provide a framework for a doctoral student.

A Proposal Outline

1)   Topic or title of the research.

2)   Aim of the research – a statement of the questions that the research will provide answers for.

3)   What motivates you to undertake this research . . .
   • in connection to your own studies and research so far,
   • in connection with the current state of research in this field,
   • your personal interest.

4)   What is the core body of your research material?

5)   What are the major ideas and areas of study in this field? This should include the issues and questions with which you expect to deal in developing your thesis. Refer to key scholarly works and sources.
   • What two or three scholars have published work which is important in this field?
   • How might you develop their ideas or challenge their thinking?
   • What are the gaps in knowledge?
   • What is distinctive about the approach you intend to take?

6)   Set out a provisional series of chapters, with a short paragraph explaining what issues you hope to explore in each chapter.

7)   What are going to be the main approaches (methods) with which you will engage in the research, and which ones will you use?

8)   Bibliography (list at least thirty scholarly books which are key to your research topic and which you expect to use).

9)   What contribution do you hope your research, when it is completed, will make to the theology and mission of the church in your home country?

Formal Assessment of the Research Proposal

Each school must determine what is expected in the development and defense of the proposal for the thesis / dissertation. This will be done in different ways. In some programs the proposal is completed before formal registration, in others it takes up a significant part of the first year of research and is part of an end-of-year review, for progression.

Usually students are unable to proceed to further years without having established a clear research outline and plan for the thesis. For dissertations of a more conceptual nature, the proposal may be fairly short, with the student showing evidence of a significant gap in the research literature that has potential to serve the church well if that gap can be addressed. In addition to showing the need for the research, the student should also show that he/ she has been able to identify relevant fields of research that will need to be explored to address the identified issue(s), and has access to the needed resources to accomplish the task. The logical argument for the study, and proposed methodology and resources needed to address the issues under investigation, are critical to the eventual success of the research effort. It is not enough to show the need, the student must show how the need can and will be addressed.

For dissertations that involve empirical research, the proposal may be a much longer document, requiring considerably more time investment. This kind of proposal will show the need for the study and potential benefits if it is carried out, a thorough review of relevant social science theory and research literature that inform the proposed research effort, preferably some theological review work relevant to the topic, and a detailed plan for the research approach, methods, sample, data collection, and analysis. Since the literature review is the initial work that is undertaken, proposals for this kind of dissertation may be one hundred or more pages in length and take up to a year or more to develop and defend before the student carries out their own empirical research work.

The Thesis / Dissertation Proposal Defense in the USA-Type Doctorate

In this type of program, the supervisor / chair of the dissertation committee oversees the proposal development process, which leads to a formal dissertation proposal defense. The chair ensures that committee members have an opportunity to review drafts of the various sections of the proposal and provide feedback to both the chair and the student regarding any areas they see needing additional work. Often, the chair will work with the student to get initial drafts completed and determine when the drafts seem to be developed well enough to share with the other committee members for their review. This process continues cyclically until the needed revisions become fewer and less extensive, signalling that with a little more work the proposal may be ready to defend. Any major concerns should be shared with the chair and student, and dealt with in the proposal development process, not saved for the proposal defense meeting. If the student is attentive to the feedback of all of the committee members, the defense should be an experience of affirmation and fine-tuning of the proposal, not a question of whether or not it should move forward at all.

After the proposal document has been submitted to the committee members in preparation for the defense meeting, the chair should meet with the student to discuss how to prepare for the defense. This should include discussing how the presentation will be made, the amount of time allotted for the presentation, the relevant information to include, any materials to share with those present (e.g. PowerPoint, handouts), and the kind of questions to be prepared to address in the interaction with the committee members (e.g. common questions given the type of dissertation research proposed). Along with this kind of guidance, prayer together for a fruitful session is always appropriate. This is a time for learning, and ensuring that the plan for the research is a strong one. Often, issues emerge in a final review of the proposal that can make it stronger, and this is an opportunity to fine-tune the proposal.

Before the proposal defense meeting begins, the committee chair may find it helpful to meet briefly with the other committee members to discuss the main issues they think need to be explored in the defense, and determine who will take the lead in raising and addressing them after the student's presentation. While not critical to the defense experience, it can help the chair to be prepared to guide the session, ensuring that each committee member is heard from, and critical issues are addressed well.

A dissertation proposal defense meeting in the US context is typically a public event open to others of the academic community to attend, both faculty and students. An announcement of the defense is typically shared with the academic community and a copy of the dissertation proposal may be made available in the doctoral program office for anyone to review. The proposal defense meeting may begin with an oral presentation of the proposal by the student, then move into a discussion of the written proposal by the committee members with the student, eventually opening up to questions and comments from others present. This meeting may take a couple of hours. The chair of the dissertation committee needs to carefully guide the process, ensuring that the discussion keeps properly focused on the proposal and things that may make it clearer, more thorough, and stronger for the accomplishment of the goals of the research.

Once the discussion is concluded, the committee may dismiss the students, faculty, and other guests present so they can have their final deliberations before reaching a decision regarding the proposed research. Choices often fall into four categories: (1) Unconditional pass, (2) Pass with minor revisions, (3) Major revisions needed and another defense held, or (4) Failure. Both options 1 and 4 would be rare, with most defenses resulting in a decision for option 2, and on rare occasions option 3. In this case, the committee must decide what revisions are needed, and who on the committee will be responsible to review and approve those revisions. In some cases, all committee members may wish to see a revision, in other cases it may be left to the chair or another reader to review and approve.

Following the proposal defense, once the student has received the decision of the committee, the chair typically meets with the student to review any revisions requested, sets a timeline for those to be addressed, and identifies who will be reviewing and approving them. The decision is also clarified as to the priority of items that need to be addressed, and what must be completed before the student moves any further into the research effort.

Case Study

Rose produced a solid piece of work at masters level, and has applied for doctoral studies. There was a bit of discussion at the admissions committee about whether she was capable of original thinking, but it was decided to let her have a chance. Rose is now working on her research proposal, yet doesn't seem to have any clear ideas on what she wants to research within her general field. As her supervisor, you have lots of ideas yourself, but you don't know if it is right to share these with Rose. You know it needs to be her own research project, not yours.

Questions

What general issues does this raise?

How should you help Rose?

Further Reading

Murray, R. *How to Write a Thesis*. Maidenhead: Open University, 2002.

Phillips, E. M., and D. S. Pugh. *How to Get a PhD: A Handbook for Students and Their Supervisors*. Maidenhead: Open University Press, 2010. (Kindle edition available also.)

Potter, S. *Doing Postgraduate Research*. London: Sage, 2006.

Smith, K. *Writing and Research: A Guide for Theological Students*. Carlisle: Langham Global Library, 2015

Taylor, S., and N. Beasley. *A Handbook for Doctoral Supervisors*. New York: Routledge, 2005.

Wisker, G. *The Good Supervisor: Supervising Postgraduate and Undergraduate Research for Doctoral Theses and Dissertations*. New York: Palgrave MacMillan, 2005.

9

Managing Doctoral Supervision Sessions

The details of supervisory relationships are a matter of individual negotiation between supervisor and student, but doctoral programs should have in place appropriate guidelines that establish the normal frequency and expected length of duration of supervisory sessions. These avoid misunderstandings about the level of support available, and create realistic expectations.[1]

The frequency of meetings will vary according to whether the student is full-time, or part-time, and the stage of the program the student has reached. At an early stage it may be necessary to meet a full-time student every week to establish the supervisory process, and the initial direction of the project. Thereafter, at least once a month for the rest of the first year is usual. In the second year the meetings will be less frequent, but should not normally be more than two months apart.

Part-time students should expect to be seen three or four times a year. Where distance is a factor, various formats such as video conferencing, Skype, etc., can be used to supplement personal face-to-face meetings. These have a different dynamic, but have been used effectively in many cases.

Setting the Outline

At an early stage set out with the student:

- How often you expect to meet. There should be institutional guidelines in place, but it is important to set out in writing what will be the practice with each individual student. There will be variations, but there should at least be a baseline frequency.

---

1. Shaw, *Best Practice*, Section 16.

- What will be the focus of the meetings? It is not always necessary to wait for a piece of work to be submitted before arranging a supervisory meeting. There should also be opportunities for monitoring, evaluation and problem solving.
- Also you need to set out the procedure for what will happen if you as supervisor are away, unwell, or on research leave.

Contact between the Formal Meetings

As a supervisor, you need to establish at an early stage what sort of contact between the formal supervisory sessions is allowed. Will informal contact be permitted or encouraged?

- How will that take place? Office hours or 24/7? What are the boundaries?
- Which methods of contact are acceptable? Email, text, telephone? Can the student 'just drop by' your office at any stage?

The Working Pattern for the Supervisory Meetings

1. Starting Out

When you start supervising a student, make clear what you expect to happen during the supervisory meetings. There is a need for a balance between direction, and also freedom for the student to develop as an independent researcher.

I remember as a research student my first meeting with my supervisor, and not being sure if I was allowed to take notes during the meeting. Clarify that sort of issue with your students.

Sometimes a request is made by the student to make an audio recording of the supervisory meeting. You will need to decide your own policy on this, but any recording should only be done with your permission, and you may wish to give instructions on how it may, or may not, be used.

2. Setting Guidelines

Set guidelines on when work needs to be submitted for review in time for you to read it, and make meaningful comments. Some students have unrealistic expectations. Most supervisors will not be able to read, comment and give directions on a 20,000 word section of text submitted the night before a supervisory meeting. Students don't always grasp that. Make clear how far in advance the work must come in, and the sort of notice you require.

3. Offering Feedback

Supervisors offer feedback in a variety of ways.

You need to explain to the student your approach in responding to written submissions. Will you produce a full report, notes on the script, electronic comments, etc.? It is best practice to give feedback in written form – verbal feedback can reinforce this, but it is not sufficient on its own.

You also need to explain to the student what they are expected to do with the feedback you have given. Should the student go back and revise the submission until all the suggested comments have been acted upon, or are they left for another day?

Students may want to quickly move on to something else, and see making revisions of drafts as dead time. However, if revisions are not made when the topic is fresh in the student's mind, they can easily be forgotten, or not acted on. It also reduces the time needed for 'writing up' at the end of the research if early drafts are well revised and updated. It can be very frustrating for a supervisor to be sent a later draft of the chapter and to find all the problems and issues identified earlier have not been addressed, and there is a need to repeat the same feedback again.

Do they hear what you are saying?

There are significant cultural issues relating to communication in student–supervisor relationships. In some cultures, supervisors will be very straightforward, direct, even blunt in their comments. Some students appreciate this clarity. Others feel discouraged, crushed, or even offended by it.

In other cultures, academic language is understated. This is especially the case in Britain where I have done much supervision, and where students have to 'read between the lines', and pick up the clues.

So, for instance, a supervisor might say:

- 'I think that there is some unevenness of quality in some sections of your work' – which means, 'You really need to improve the quality of those areas because it is not good.'
- 'You should look more closely at what that writer says' – which means, 'You have totally misunderstood what that author said.'
- 'This section needs more clarity' – means, 'This section is unclear, confused and does not make sense.'
- 'I would advise you get the help of a proofreader' – means, 'your work is littered with grammatical and spelling errors and the examiner will fail it if you submit it as it is.'

Problems occur when the culture of the supervisor and that of the student clash, and the student misreads the signals. I was struck by hearing of an American student asking an opinion of his nearly completed draft thesis from his supervisor who was an English gentleman of the old school.

'Well, sir,' said the student, 'Tell me straight, is it rubbish or not? (He may in fact have used a less delicate expression, which I will not repeat) I just want to know.' To which the kindly man replied, 'I think there are some areas that need some attention.'

Instead of reading this as a warning that significant work was still needed, the American student understood this to mean that he only needed to make some minor revisions, which he did. He submitted his thesis, and was failed.

Watch carefully what you are communicating to students, and how they are receiving it. Make sure that your direction and instruction is clear, and students do not need to 'read between the lines'. When working with students from other cultures this is especially important. You may need to get students to repeat back to you their understanding of what has been said. The issues you are communicating about are too important to be misunderstood over.

4. Keeping a Record of Discussions and Comments

A record should be kept of the time and location of each supervisory meeting, even an informal one, and the main points of advice and direction given. These will be used in major reports. They are also an important record should a complaint about the nature of the supervision ever be made.

It is common now for the supervisor to ask the student to produce a report of the meeting, and send it to you, with the issues discussed, decisions made, and directions given. This serves as a record, and also a check to ensure the student has understood what has been asked of them.

The Types of Supervisory Meetings

1. Ad Hoc

These are usually brief, and focus on a specific issue. Maybe a student needs to check a reference, or get some basic information. It may be at the end of a seminar, or even in the corridor. There is no need to keep a record of these meetings.

2. Informal Meetings

These may take the form of a general discussion or update on progress, without a piece of work being discussed. Maybe a piece of work is in process, and some aspects need to be considered. These meetings could be by Skype, email, or telephone, etc.

A written note of these meetings should be kept as a record, and the student can draft some notes which the supervisor confirms. These are used in more formal reports.

3. Formal Meetings

This is the forum where formal feedback to a piece of work is given.

Such meetings may be needed to help prepare for a specific review stage, or a progression upgrade. In some formal meetings there is value in stepping back and looking at sections of the text to assess the big picture of overall progression being made, and plans for completion. In the final year of study, a plan needs to be in place and agreed for completion of the thesis.

4. Progress Reviews

On most programs there will normally be at least one formal meeting a year where the progress and continuation of the student on the program is discussed, and any issues relating to upgrade and transfer of registration are resolved, or permission given for students to submit work for examination. These reports should be prepared by the student and supervisor. The meeting will involve other participants than the student and supervisor, and is likely to include the Program Leader, or head of department. Formal records need to be kept of decisions, and these communicated to the student in writing.

Setting the Supervisory Styles

It is important that the student understands your supervisory style at an early point. I have come across some supervisors who adopt a 'one size fits all' policy, and who effectively say, 'this is my style, and you either adapt to it or find another supervisor'. While we will want to use the skills and experience we have in a way that we are comfortable with, an inflexible approach is not always helpful. There are occasions when adaptability is a virtue.

Again, it is good to discuss your supervisory style at an early stage with your students.

Reflective Questions

Reflect on your own supervisory style. How would you describe it?

What approaches are you able to change?

What aspects are you not prepared to change? If not, why not?

Are there occasions when you have used different styles with different students?

What were those different styles, and what issues were you seeking to address with the student?

Styles of Supervision That Tend to Be Used

1. Direct Active

This is a very engaged style, carefully telling the student what they must do at each stage, and what not to do. The process is carefully controlled, and the student knows exactly what is expected of them. While this can be helpful with students who lack confidence, or have little experience of working independently, it creates a strong sense of dependency which works against the creativity and independence that the doctoral process requires. At the end of the process, a student should be a self-managing learner, but this approach is unlikely to achieve that. It may be necessary to adopt this approach at early stages of a project, or with weaker students who are struggling, but it is very demanding on the supervisor.

2. Indirect Active

This approach sees more engagement with student's own thinking. They are consciously drawn into planning the next stages of work. The supervisor regularly asks, what do you think is the next step you should take? Students are invited to review their own work and its progress. The supervisor will ask – in which areas do you think the work needs to be developed? So the supervisor is clearly guiding the process, but making sure that the student offers answers and solutions to the issues.

3. Indirect Passive

Here the student clearly takes the lead, and the supervisor's role is to support, listen, and respond when asked. The student usually comes with a series of questions or answers they want advice and support with, or ideas and hypotheses they want to test out. At these moments the student is becoming the self-managing learner, and using academic advice in a discerning manner. Supervisors need to make sure that they continue to 'steer' the project back onto the right course if wrong directions appear to be taken, or progress is not being made quickly enough, but student ownership and motivation is high. With some highly active and energetic students, the supervisory intervention needed is to tell them to attempt less, to more narrowly delimit the field, and not be overambitious.

4. Passive

In this approach the supervisor is purely responsive, and offers little or no direction. The view is that it is the student's project, they should lead it, and the supervisor simply responds to work that is sent, if any. In my experience of supporting doctoral students in a variety of contexts, this is the approach that students complain about the most, and find most difficult to handle, especially early in their project. When they discuss the possible fields they may explore, the supervisor simply says 'it's your project, it's up to you', or 'it's not my role to offer that sort of direction'. Some students have presented a series of research proposals only to be told 'that won't work, try another approach', without any direction being offered as to the approach that should take. In some institutions and academic contexts, this approach is surprisingly common. However, this does not work with quite a lot of students, and yields high levels of student dissatisfaction and even resentment – 'why am I paying such large fees when my supervisor gives me no idea of what I should be doing'. I have seen a number of students drop out in the face of extreme supervisor passivity, which often looks more like indifference. At the later stages of the PhD the supervisory mode may well become more responsive than directive, but generally to sit and wait for students to deliver work and only respond to what is sent is not a good model throughout the full duration of thesis writing.

I would advocate adaptability in style, changing it as the project develops. Generally the style may progress from being more directive to less directive. Students work in different ways, and at different paces, and even in the doctorate will have different ability levels.

Don't let projects drift for a long time if the student is not making headway. If one approach is not working, then another should be attempted.

Reflective Questions

From your own experience, what was your own doctoral supervisor's style?

What were the three most effective things your supervisor did in supervisory sessions with you?

What were the three least effective things your supervisor did?

Educating Students to Get the Most from Supervision

The 'rules of engagement' for doctoral supervision need to be clear.

To enable the student to get the most from supervision, some factors are important:

i)   Help students see that supervision is a collaborative effort. It is not just about them receiving feedback, but about you and the student working together.

ii) Students must learn independence, and as the research project develops to be encouraged to take a lead. By the end of the doctoral process they should not always be asking, 'What do I do next?'

iii)   Let the relationship grow and develop. Over time you should become less directive, and be more of a dialogue partner. By the end of the process you will be academic peers, and maybe, some day, colleagues.

iv)   Make sure the student understands the need to present well-edited work so time is not wasted working on basic spelling, grammatical, presentational and stylistic issues.

v)   Students need to know what their responsibilities are – concerning punctuality, communication, preparation, information flow.

vi)   Be aware that as well as the supervisor managing the supervisory relationship, there will be an element in which the student needs to 'manage' the supervisor. In my own experience of being supervised there were elements of my supervisor's approach that I needed to work my way round and manage to ensure the supervisory meeting accomplished what I needed.

A very accessible guide to the doctoral process is E. M. Phillips and D. S. Pugh, *How to Get a PhD*.[2] It includes many instructive and challenging examples. One very helpful chapter is entitled 'How to Manage Your Supervisor', which is good for both students and supervisors to read, to understand the dynamics of the relationship.

The Relationship You Want to Be Established

A key question you should ask is, Is this a business relationship, or a friendship relationship?

This affects the type of feedback you will give, and the way the meetings are conducted. It will affect how you address the student, and how you want them to address you. Is it first name terms, or is it 'Dr Shaw'? National and institutional culture will affect how you handle this. My supervisor was a very senior figure, nearing retirement, and I never felt it appropriate to use his first name in addressing him.

Remember good supervision can take place even if you don't really get on well with the person you are supervising! Professional respect and a desire to bring the best from the student should override how we feel. But also remember, lasting friendships and mentoring relationships can grow out of good supervision. You are building the next generation of scholars. Through the process the student should be enthused, inspired, supported and feel valued and cared for.

---

2. Phillips and Pugh, *How to Get a PhD*.

The Pastoral Dimension of Supervision

In chapter 3 I listed the aspects of supervision style that doctoral students reacted to most positively when I discussed this with them. In this the pastoral dimension came out as very important. There is much more to the student before you than the work they are presenting and discussing. Their emotional, physical, and spiritual well being will affect their capacity to function well in their studies. There will be issues in their family life that impinge on their research work. Similarly in their community there will be stresses and challenges. I worked with one student who was studying away from home, and his country was invaded by hostile forces in the middle of his doctorate. Another student's homeland suffered a military coup, and another a devastating typhoon. In all this, the capacity to demonstrate genuine pastoral concern for them as a whole person is very significant.

It is very important for the doctoral supervisor to have a pastoral heart and pastoral capabilities, as the ICETE *Best Practice Guidelines* highlight. Yet the supervisor is not the student's pastor, nor is the primary role of the supervisor to offer pastoral advice. Showing pastoral sensitivity and concern is important, but for in-depth pastoral support or counseling the student should be directed to a chaplain, a pastoral tutor or a qualified counsellor, or their own church where pastoral ministry is provided. There is usually insufficient time in supervisory meetings to offer extensive pastoral support, and there is a danger it can interfere with the academic and training elements of supervision. So pastoral awareness and sensitivity is vital, but when significant pastoral issues arise, it is wise to refer the student on to the appropriate specialists.

I tend to spend the first few minutes of a supervisory session asking how a student is, and how their family are, noting any issues that arise that might affect their progress, or need further attention – and make sure they are directed to the appropriate support mechanisms for any help they need. But this should not be prolonged beyond what is necessary, and the primary focus of academic supervision should be maintained. Many supervisors begin and / or end a supervisory session with prayer, asking for God's help and blessing on the student and the next step in their studies.

Many students have appreciated the opportunity to visit a supervisor's home for coffee, or for a meal. Opening yourself up to students personally, and showing hospitality, is a way of modeling the spiritual formation we seek. But there need to be appropriate limits, and some supervisors are concerned that too much personal contact outside supervisory meetings can affect their ability to offer detailed and objective critique of the student's work. The appropriate checks and balances need to be kept in place.

Problem Areas in Supervisory Sessions

1)   The supervisor talks too much.

In this scenario, the supervisory session becomes a lecture, with no dialogue. There is no room for student engagement or the development of student initiative or leadership.

There is only one person who can redress this situation!

Reflect on your own practice, and assess the balance in the meeting between the student contributions and your own. Does anything need to change?

2)   The student talks too much.

This is equally problematic, because the supervisor is unable to communicate vital information, or give direction. It is also not good practice if the student eventually needs to undergo an oral examination. Examiners will be very frustrated if students cannot answer questions clearly and precisely, and talk all the time. Clear direction and handling is needed to ensure proper balance is sustained.

3)   The student is reluctant to say much, or to ask and answer questions.

Silence on the part of the student may be their own fault, not that of the supervisor.

In these cases the student needs to be drawn out so that they learn how to confidently and clearly talk about their own work. Again, this is a vital skill to learn for an oral examination, and also for academic presentations or future lessons.

Giving preparatory directions to the student about what they will be asked to discuss or answer questions about in a forthcoming supervisory session will build expectation and confidence with students.

4)   The student comes but is not prepared.

This does occasionally happen, but if it becomes a repeated pattern it needs to be challenged. Where a student is not prepared, supervision meetings should be kept short, and rearranged for when the student is prepared. It is inconsiderate of a student to arrange a meeting and use your time, without putting in the time to prepare, or doing you the courtesy of contacting you in advance to move the meeting to another time.

The issues faced by doctoral students vary from one supervisor to another, and from one institution to another. In the European-based PhD model, the supervisory relationship usually sees the doctoral student relating closely to one or two people. In the US-based doctorate, the relationship is usually with a committee. This create a different series of challenges

Common Challenges with USA-Style PhD Dissertation Committees and Ways to Address Them

Disagreement between Committee Members

It is not uncommon for dissertation committee members to have differing ideas and standards for the work they expect from the dissertation student. This is why it is important for the dissertation committee chair to discuss the student's proposed research focus with committee members early in the process, striving to come to a common understanding of the research product anticipated. Where possible, a meeting of the full committee with the student early on for an initial discussion of the proposed research can help orient the full group regarding what they can expect, and each can speak into the project, voicing what they would see as important to address or include.

As drafts of portions of the dissertation are shared with various committee members, it is important that the chair receive any feedback from committee members before it is shared with the student. This allows the chair to identify any areas of conflict in expectations and talk with the other committee members to resolve the areas of disagreement or differing perspective. The goal should be for the committee to work through these issues together without dragging the student into the middle of it. A thorough process of review of drafts should surface any major differences among the committee members, allowing time to work them out before a public proposal defense or final defense is held.

If there are major disagreements that emerge early in the committee's work, and they cannot be resolved, there should be a way by which a committee member can quietly leave the committee and another member be recruited. The chair will want to discuss this kind of situation with the director of the doctoral program to ensure that this is handled in a way that preserves good working relationships among colleagues. If a major disagreement develops at the dissertation final defense, and it cannot be resolved within the meeting, it may be best for the vote of the members to be delayed, allowing time for another meeting of the committee (with or without the student) to work through the issues. This should be an extremely rare occurrence, and if good review and communication is done before the defense it should not happen.

Slow Responses from Second and Third Readers

Schools should set expectations as to how much time committee members should take in reviewing drafts of documents sent to them. This expectation should then be clearly communicated both to the faculty members who serve on the committee, and to the student. Students will then know how long they should wait before enquiring about the status of a review, and faculty members will know the deadlines they should be submitting their comments by.

If the chair notes that a committee member has a pattern of taking more time than expected to complete reviews and submit feedback, and this is delaying the student's work, the chair should contact the committee member to discuss the cause for the delays and re-emphasize the importance of timely feedback and the expected deadlines. In many cases there are things outside of the control of the committee member that may be creating challenges and patience will be needed. In other cases, the committee member may simply have lost track of the deadline and a simple reminder will get them back on track. The chair can help keep the review process from bogging down; reducing the stress the student would face due to long delays.

Perceptions from Doctoral Students of What Effective Supervision Looks Like

The list below comes from students who have expressed their appreciation of various aspects of supervision, and it serves as an effective checklist of what to aspire to. Each supervisor will develop their own style, but the following gives a list of key indicators:

1) Adaptability to the developing needs of the student at different stages of the project.

2) Adaptability to different students' learning styles.

3) Ability to read the cues from the students. If the student is asking, 'What do I do next?' – have you encouraged too much dependency or do they need more support than you have given?

4) Being able to set boundaries as to what the supervisor is able and not able to do.

5) Providing structure to the student's progress and work, making sure proper planning takes place.

6) Being able to draw out the strengths of others in the supervisory team.

7) Showing respect to the student and interest in their work.

8) Ability to give feedback that students can understand, and respond to with appropriate action.

9) Willingness to give students broader training and mentored support, such as doing some lecturing, grading scripts, etc.

10) Giving instruction on specific methodological and research ethics issues.

11) Creating an environment in which discussion as well as exchange of ideas can take place.

12) Teaching students to be self-critical of their own work.

13) Building from short-term goals, to longer-term goals and the bigger picture.

14) Showing you have read the student's work – a comment on a page, or a tick at the bottom – avoids the comments that students make about supervisors not being bothered to read their work.

15) Pointing the student to proper institutional support when facing problems, such as library, administrative, finance, etc.

16) Assisting students with writing and preparation of conference papers.

17) Building morale. Showing confidence in the student's work and praising signs of progress, dealing with demoralization and demotivation.

18) Maintaining proper professional judgment – it does a struggling student no favors to prolong the agony of failure, even if they are very likeable as a person.

19) Be aware that you are a role model – what you do to your students, they may well do to others!

Further Reading

Eley, A. and R. Murray, *How to Be an Effective Supervisor*. Maidenhead: Open University Press, 2009.

Gatfield, T. 'An Investigation into PhD Supervisory Management Styles', *Journal of Higher Education Policy and Management*, Vol. 27, No. 3, November 2005, 311–325.

Murray, R. *How to Write a Thesis*. Maidenhead: Open University Press, 2002.

Phillips, E. M. and D. S. Pugh. *How to Get a PhD: A Handbook for Students and Their Supervisors*. Maidenhead: Open University Press, 2010. (Kindle edition available also.)

Shaw, I. *Best Practice Guidelines for Doctoral Programs*. Carlisle: Langham Global Library, 2015.

Taylor, Stan, and N. Beasley. *A Handbook for Doctoral Supervisors*. New York: Routledge, 2005.

Wisker, Gina. *The Good Supervisor: Supervising Postgraduate and Undergraduate Research for Doctoral Theses and Dissertations*. New York: Palgrave MacMillan, 2005.

10

Excellence in Academic Research Supervision and Spiritual Formation

Doctoral study within an evangelical Christian institution is founded on an understanding of knowledge that is more than academic. In the Bible, acquiring and exercising wisdom involves a combination of faith, reason and action. It requires:

- *right belief and committed trust in the living God ('the fear of the LORD is the first principle of wisdom'),*
- *creative and humble use of the rationality God has granted to humans made in his own image, and*
- *appropriate living in the world to reflect God's calling and participate in God's mission.*

ICETE, *Beirut Benchmarks*, Preamble

In whatever context it is undertaken, PhD study is about both learning and being. Doctoral study is an aspect of transformative learning, and the task of making meaning (in the doctorate out of the sources and data we encounter in research), is connected to our intrinsic spirituality. Research is more than a cold exercise in rationalistic analysis, it draws on imagination, intuition and emotion even in the most secular of contexts. Doctoral study should impact the cognitive, social, and affective dimensions of personhood. In evangelical institutions, supervisors need to create an environment in which students are engaged at all these levels. This personal growth goes far beyond the academic analysis of theological concepts. Through the experience of being supervised students should come away with an enhanced sense of self-worth, with deeper abilities to construct meaning and knowledge. This is how the ICETE *Best Practice Guidelines* express this:

> Doctoral programs should encourage scholars to see the connection between research work and spiritual formation. Researchers should seek integration

of both academic and spiritual excellence, working to the higher end of the
transformation of the whole people of God according to the image of Christ
and his mission in the world.[1]

Alongside the capacity for advanced theological reflection, doctoral students need to
continue to grow in spiritual awareness, moral judgment, wisdom, maturity of character,
and understanding of their faith community. Many doctoral students are preparing
for work in a theological college, seminary, or Bible school. Others will take strategic
leadership roles in Christian ministry. In offering doctoral training, encouraging
spiritual formation needs to feature strongly in the missional purpose of the supervisor
of doctoral students, and this should mould how we approach the task. That makes this
chapter probably the most important in this book.

Spiritual formation has been defined as 'the intentional processes by which the
marks of an authentic Christian spirituality are formed and integrated.'[2] The heart of
Christian spirituality is not just knowing about the eternal God, but knowing him first-
hand through the Lord Jesus Christ. The process of preparing a person for an aspect of
Christian ministry, including strategic leadership in theological education or the church,
should serve to deepen that knowledge of God. So, alongside progress in academic
formation, the process of undertaking doctoral studies in an evangelical institution
should be marked by a deeper commitment to Christ; greater reverence and faithfulness
towards his Word; stronger appreciation for our neighbor; and deeper integration in
the church community. Sadly, for some students, the opposite of all these appears to be
the outcome of the process of doctoral study. In the research doctorate, where academic
study is of the highest level, and pressures the most intense, the tendency to push to the
margins the pursuit of an integral life of faith are great.

Constant contact by theological students with the things of God brings the danger
that the priests and Levites faced in the Old Testament, that of the sacred becoming
reduced to the commonplace and customary. The Bible is littered with examples of how
dangerous this was – we only need to ask Uzzah about that! The privilege of handling
the most profound of things should never be lost. As one of the great theologians at
Princeton put it over a century ago:

> Are you, by this constant contact with divine things, growing in holiness,
> becoming every day more and more [people] of God? If not, you are
> hardening! You will never prosper in your religious life in the theological
> seminary until your work in the theological seminary becomes itself to you

---

1. Shaw, *Best Practice*, Section 8.

2. S. Amirtham, and R. Pryor, eds., *The Invitation to the Feast of Life; Resources for Spiritual Formation in Theological Education* (Geneva: World Council of Churches, 1991).

a religious exercise out of which you draw every day enlargement of heart, elevation of spirit, and adoring delight in your Maker and your Saviour.[3]

The Culture of Theological Education

In the desire for evangelical theological colleges and seminaries to gain academic credibility, and for students to graduate from their courses with qualifications and credentials, there has necessarily been a stress on the academic dimensions of theology. This emphasis on the training of the mind led Lesslie Newbigin to speak of the 'Babylonian Captivity of theological education' by academia, exiling theology from the life and needs of churches.[4] Intensely detailed biblical or theological study can be undertaken which has little relevance to the understanding of the whole biblical text, or the person of God, or to the church or Christian life and witness.

The tendency for doctoral student and supervisor to concentrate on the cultivation of the mind, and the failure to integrate that with the ongoing need for spiritual formation, can leave doctoral students struggling with a sense of profound disconnection between their academic work, and their personal relationship with God, or their connection with their local church community. Students are longing for good role models in this area.

Models for Promoting Spiritual Formation

Our model for the perfect theological educator is of course Jesus. He spent around three formative years with his disciples instilling in them his teaching, but also the pattern for how to live and think, how to 'be' his followers, and integrate the two. He taught them consistency of belief and practice. Peter could boldly proclaim undying loyalty to Jesus, but what really mattered was how he behaved in the ordinary circumstances of the life of faith. A serious disconnection between proclamation and practice came after Jesus had been arrested, and he was questioned round the fireside by a range of people including a servant girl. However, he demonstrated a strong connectivity between belief and practice in his amazing sermon at the day of Pentecost. Those three years of investing in the theological education of his disciples produced a group of followers who not only were willing to spend and be spent in an extraordinary period of mission which, before they died, had touched most of the countries of the Middle East and the Mediterranean basin, but had also faithfully passed on the most profound expression of doctrine and practice of their master to the next generation.

---

3. B. B. Warfield, *The Religious Life of Theological Students*, lecture given at Autumn Conference at Princeton Theological Seminary, October 4, 1911.

4. Quoted in David Heywood, 'A New Paradigm for Theological Education?' *Anvil* 17, no. 1 (2000): 19.

Your Own Experience of Being Mentored in Academic Excellence and Spiritual Formation

As we saw when looking at supervisory approaches, we tend to default to basing our practice on our own experience. If PhD study was undertaken in the context of a secular university, it may not be so easy to derive a model to be repeated from our experience, although a number of evangelical supervisors in those contexts find ways to model the principles we are seeking to promote.

Reflective Questions

How did your supervisor / mentor model the connection between research and spiritual formation?

How did your supervisor / mentor fail to model the connection between research and spiritual formation?

What key lessons do you derive from your own past experience?

The Experience of Others

During training seminars I have run for doctoral supervisors, I often ask the participants what they understand by 'spiritual formation'. Here are a few of their answers:

- Concern for the whole person
- Integration of knowledge and being
- Worship
- Developing values
- Shaping world views
- Relationship with God

Reflective Questions

What do you think of these responses?

What do you think is the best definition of spiritual formation?

Things Supervisors Are Commended for When Promoting Spiritual Formation

In training seminars I also ask what things that the doctoral supervisors did to promote spiritual formation that were good, as well as the things they did not do well.

Good things were . . .
- Being sincere, committed Christians;
- Involved in church ministry;
- Respect for the individual;
- Respect for the views of others, even if they disagree with them;
- Academic integrity reflected their integrity as persons;
- 'Genuine' people;
- Humility before the truth.

Less good things were . . .
- 'Did not pray with me';
- 'Very reserved';
- 'It never became a friendship';
- Lack of sharing about their own spiritual life.

Then I ask participants in the seminars how they want to promote the integration of spiritual formation and academic excellence. Here are some comments made:
- Stress that academic excellence glorifies God;
- Stress how academic excellence reflects spirituality;
- Heart, mind and soul need to be in study;
- Academic work is an expression of service and love to God;
- Humility should be demonstrated;
- Seeking knowledge is a spiritual act;
- Helping students learn by unlearning, and setting aside prejudices;
- Not avoiding the big and difficult questions;
- Theology is about your life – it is a verb – you live it, do it;
- Make sure there is some relevant service to the church / community.

Reflective Questions

Write down your feelings about these types of responses.

What surprises you?

The key question that supervisors need to address is, how do we do this, or do it better?

What We Are Seeking to Form in Our Doctoral Students

John Stott identified training the faculty of evangelical theological institutions as key for the future of the church, a concern that led him to found the Langham Partnership Scholarship program: 'Seminary teachers are the key personnel, as they influence for good or ill generation after generation of the church's future clergy. What is needed, then, is a steady stream of new faculty members who combine academic excellence with personal godliness.'[5]

So what does this 'personal godliness' that the supervisor is to inculcate, look like?

1. Faithfulness to Christ

This of course is what Jesus did with his disciples, such that after three years in his company they were prepared not only to turn the world upside down, but also to die for him. Future theological faculty should be trained to be Christocentric – working to honor and please the Lord Jesus Christ in everything.

> Whatever you do, work at it with all your heart, as working for the Lord.
> (Col 3:23)

As Dietrich Bonhoeffer puts it in *Life Together*, (his model for the theological seminary), 'Work, which takes up the bulk of the day, is given a sense of meaning and unity when it is done – in the name of the Lord Jesus.'[6]

2. Faithfulness to God's Word

> *Researchers should be faithful both to the Word of God and the demands of their discipline.*[7]

As Dietrich Bonhoeffer notes, only in Scripture do we learn to understand reality correctly. We sit at the feet of the Lord, and listen to his voice, and his agenda becomes our agenda.[8] Theological study should regularly shift over into doxology.

3. Faithfulness in Prayer

Doctoral students need to be, and to remain, people of prayer. They need metaphorically to study on their knees. They should not be ashamed to pray over aspects of their research, indeed they should be encouraged to invite God into the dynamics of what they

---

5. John Stott in a letter to friends, March 1994.
6. D. Bonhoeffer, *Life Together* (London, SCM, 1954), 54.
7. Shaw, *Best Practice*, Section 8.
8. Bonhoeffer, *Life Together*, 56.

are doing. Conversation with God can be a place for critical self-reflection and critical discourse. This is how B. B. Warfield spoke of this aspect of integration:

> If we face the tremendous difficulty of the work before us, it will certainly throw us back upon our knees; and if we worthily gauge the power of the gospel committed to us, that will certainly keep us on our knees.[9]

Bonhoeffer called his students to commit one another into the hands of God with prayers for blessing, peace, and preservation . . . petition of forgiveness for wrongs done.[10]

4. Faithfulness to Community

> *The important role that community plays in the formation of scholars should be recognised in doctoral programs.*[11]

Much of modern spirituality is individualistic, in contrast to the emphasis on community in the New Testament. We tend to emphasize the 'what we make of it' dimensions of community, and forget that through it we are entering into something God has created. Christianity means community through Jesus Christ and in Jesus Christ. Apart from Christ, Christian community does not exist and has no purpose. God invites Christians into what he is doing in the community of his people. As Bonhoeffer puts it, 'We belong to one another only through and in Jesus Christ.'[12] Worshiping together is an expression, and an outcome, of community, and should be attended by both faculty and students in evangelical institutions where doctoral programs are offered.

Doctoral study is best done in community. This involves:

1) Patiently, attentively, listening to others. This takes place in discussions, training seminars, during academic presentations. It is an aspect of loving your neighbor, and love to the community. Supervisors need to teach scholars to respect the views of other scholars, even if they don't agree with them. They need models for how to debate and disagree graciously, and in a spirit of humble learning. Doctoral students should support and uphold their fellow students in the academic community, encouraging them by attending their presentations at research seminars and asking meaningful questions. Students need to realize that the academic failings such as plagiarism are a failure to love neighbor.

---

9. Warfield, *Theological Students*, 192.
10. Bonhoeffer, *Life Together,* 58–61.
11. Shaw, *Best Practice Guidelines,* Section 4.
12. Bonhoeffer, *Life Together*, 21.

2)   The virtue of helpfulness. In community, scholars learn to work with and for each other. Whether with a computer problem, a missing reference, locating a source, the need for a mutual support network is vital. Marriage partners of different students might wish to share childcare. Helpfulness is needed in small and large ways.

3)   Bearing burdens. In the doctoral program I ran we regularly held research community lunches and prayer times. The ability of students to share and pray for each other was very significant. If one was struggling, or feeling like giving up, or another had illness in the family, then the rest of the group could encourage and pray for them.

As Paul put it in 1 Thessalonians, all this is an outworking of love for one another.

> Now concerning love of brothers and sisters . . . you yourselves have been taught by God to love one another. . . . But we urge you, brothers and sisters, to do so more and more. (1 Thess 4:9–10)

5. Faithfulness to the Church

Warfield observed how through engagement with a local church, and community worship within the institution, students would draw out 'a support and inspiration for your personal religious life which you can get nowhere else, and which you cannot afford to miss.'[13]

6. Faithfulness to Their Calling

B. B. Warfield reminded his students of the reason for their studies:

> You are gathered together here for a religious purpose, in preparation for the highest religious service which can be performed by men – the guidance of others in the religious life . . . as students for the ministry: Keep always before your mind the greatness of your calling, that is to say, these two things: the immensity of the task before you, the infinitude of the resources at your disposal . . .[14]

---

13. Warfield, *Theological Students*, 189.
14. Ibid., 188.

Reflective Questions

How do the 'demands of the discipline' challenge your personal commitment to biblical faithfulness?

How would you help a doctoral student reconcile the tension?

What approaches will you take to modeling and encouraging spiritual formation?

What is the goal of developing community among doctoral students?

Why do doctoral students often opt out of corporate worship opportunities and isolate themselves from the academic community?

Spiritual Formation Involves Integration

> But learning, though indispensable, is not the most indispensable thing for a minister. Before and above being learned, a minister must be godly. Nothing could be more fatal, however, than to set these two things over against one another. . . . Why should you turn from God when you turn to your books, or feel that you must turn from your books in order to turn to God?[15]

Doctoral students should be shown how to avoid the separation between their academic discipline and the rest of life, which too often characterizes advanced studies.

Reflective Questions

As a doctoral supervisor, reflect on the relationship between your own academic life and your personal spiritual development.

Are you satisfied with the interactions? What needs to change?

What difficulties in this area have you seen among colleagues?

How do you seek to integrate academic and spiritual excellence in your work with those you teach?

In what way do you believe that your role as a supervisor and researcher help to fulfil the mission of Christ in the world?

---

15. Ibid., 182–183.

It Takes a Whole Evangelical Seminary to Train a Doctoral Student

It should be emphasized that spiritual formation is the responsibility of the whole doctoral program, not just the supervisor. Also, the students themselves must be fully committed to the need for growth in the integration of academic and spiritual formation. That should be a criterion for those applying to join the doctoral program. The saying 'it takes a whole seminary to train a student' is as true here as elsewhere. Faculty, staff and students are implicated in this as part of a learning and supportive community, such that the process becomes reciprocal, and faculty and staff also grow spiritually through the interaction.

One of the reasons why a student has chosen the evangelical seminary as a context for their doctoral studies should be its commitment to holistic academic and spiritual formation. This similarly motivates the supervisor to work in that context rather than another. If there is no commitment to the spiritual formation of the student, the student may just as well study in a secular university setting. The commitment to a high quality academic research environment should be enhanced by the commitment to spiritual formation. The evangelical seminary should match what is available in the secular academy as an academic context, without losing sight of their purpose of also creating a context for advanced growth in spirituality.

The Character of the Evangelical Doctoral Supervisor

Spiritual development should is not to be isolated from academic formation, but 'it must be a perspective affecting the whole educative process.'[16] The way supervisors conduct themselves should reflect this. Key attributes include:

1. Humility

> While striving for academic excellence, doctoral programs should also be rooted in belief in the absolute necessity of humility and total dependence on God. The pursuit of knowledge through autonomous human intelligence without reliance on the Spirit of God is not God honouring. Doctoral scholars should seek God's help in all aspects of lives and their education.[17]

As the Apostle Paul puts it, let no man 'think of himself more highly than he ought to think' (Rom 12:3). In the words of Dietrich Bonhoeffer, 'He who would learn to serve

---

16. B. J. Nicholls, 'The Role of Spiritual Development in Theological Education,' *Evangelical Review of Theology* 19, no. 3 (1995): 231.

17. Shaw, *Best Practice Guidelines*, Section 8.

must first learn to think little of himself.'[18] As Thomas á Kempis wrote in *On the Imitation of Christ*, 'Of what use is it to discourse learnedly on the Trinity if you lack humility and therefore displease the Trinity?'[19]

Those who knew the great New Testament scholar F. F. Bruce often commented on the brilliance of his knowledge of both Greek and Hebrew, but also on the humility with which he shared his ideas.

Reflective Questions

Give examples of leading scholars you have known who have demonstrated such humility.

How do we deal with the tension of being academic leader, mentor and guide, while having 'no opinion of ourselves'?

---

2. Truthfulness

> *Programs should inculcate the values of honesty and intellectual rigour, a commitment to the truth wherever it leads, and a humble willingness to acknowledge mistakes, misunderstandings, prejudices and presuppositions, and value their correction.*[20]

Reflective Questions

How, as a doctoral supervisor, can you model honesty and a commitment to truth wherever it leads?

What are the difficulties as an academic leader of acknowledging mistakes, misunderstandings, presuppositions?

---

3. Ethical and Intellectual Consistency

> *Scholars and supervisors should be committed to research that will be deep and rigorous, and which demonstrates ethical and intellectual consistency.*[21]

---

18. D. Bonhoeffer, *Life Together*, ch. 4.
19. T. A Kempis, *The Imitation of Christ* (Harmondsworth, Penguin, 1952), 27.
20. Shaw, *Best Practice Guidelines*, Section 8.
21. Shaw, *Best Practice Guidelines*, Section 8.

Reflective Questions

What examples have you seen where research and teaching has lacked ethical and intellectual consistency, and what have you learned from these?

In what areas have you felt the temptation to unethical behavior or intellectual inconsistency?

4. Authenticity

Theological educators need to be in touch with their own spirituality and to be people of integrity. What they expect in those they supervise, they should be prepared to practice themselves. Students quickly recognize inconsistencies.

In 1992, ACTEA required of seminary lecturers 'an active participation in the life and worship of the institution . . . it is not merely decorative but biblically essential that the whole educational body – staff and students – not only learns together, but plays and eats and cares and worships and works together.'[22]

In sum, the qualities the supervisor needs to demonstrate and inspire in others include personal spirituality (passion for Jesus, hunger for personal godliness), vision (ability to inspire and instil vision in others), pastoral gifts, communication ability, scholarship undertaken with a servant mentality, personal transparency, love for the church, love for people.

The role of training future Christian leaders is both honorable and deeply demanding. In North America, an Association of Theological Schools' report on Spiritual Formation in 1972 concluded 'Faculty should be active in their own spiritual formation and development . . . the spiritual development and formation of students begins with and depends on the spirituality of the faculty'[23]

Much of what students learn about spiritual formation comes implicitly – through the mood-music, the attitudes, the demeanor and disposition of faculty. The relationship between teachers and students on a theological course contribute to the process of spiritual formation. Attitudes of mistrust and coldness undermine positive efforts in other directions. In one training seminar I ran, a newly qualified doctoral graduate from a major evangelical institution in North America openly spoke about the discontinuity between what faculty taught in the classroom, and how they criticized each other outside the classroom.

---

22. Accrediting Council for Theological Education in Africa, *Standards and Procedures for Accreditation at Post-secondary level*, Fifth edition (Kaduna, Nigeria: ACTEA Continental Office, 1992).

23. D. Babin, E. Briner, L. A., Hoon, P. W., Martin, W. R., Smith, T., Van Antwerp, P. J. Whitney, *Voyage-Vision-Venture: A Report by the Task Force on Spiritual Development* (Dayton: American Association of Theological Schools, 1972), 9, 27.

Spirituality is being formed constantly through interaction with students – whether in formal supervisory sessions, or seminars, or worship, or on outings, retreats, days of prayer, and communal meals. How you live and share your faith in these contexts as a supervisor is vital to students, especially those from non-Western cultures.

The Ultimate Goal

This is how Warfield sums up the aim and incredible privilege in all this:

> A minister must be both learned and religious. It is not a matter of choosing between the two. He must study, but he must study as in the presence of God and not in a secular spirit. He must recognize the privilege of pursuing his studies in the environment where God and salvation from sin are the air he breathes.[24]

Students and supervisors are called to 'grow in the grace and knowledge of our Lord Jesus Christ' (2 Pet 3:18). The role of the doctoral supervisor in the evangelical institution includes providing a context in which that can take place – where the things of God and salvation are the 'air he breathes'. This requires a holistic and integrated educational approach, not one narrowly focused on cognitive growth and academic attainment. The spiritual growth of the doctoral student should not be incidental to that, but essential and integrated. The doctoral supervisor should strive to deliver a student at the end of the program who is a number of steps nearer to completion and wholeness in Christ. Our aim is to present every person 'mature in Christ' (Col 1:28).

Reflective Questions

As a result of reading this chapter, what will you do differently in your next meeting with your students?

What two changes will you make to the way you evaluate your student's progress?

What ideas should your institution adopt to advance the spiritual formation of your doctoral students?

---

24. Warfield, *Theological Students*, 189.

Further Reading

Bonhoeffer, D. *Life Together.* London: SCM, 1954.

Cannell, L. 'Theology, Spiritual Formation and Theological Education: Reflections Toward Application.' In *Life in the Spirit Life in the Spirit: Spiritual Formation in Theological Perspective,* edited by J. P. Greenman and G. Kalantzis. Downers Grove: IVP, 2010.

Cheesman, G. 'The Spiritual Formation of Students – A Personal Selection from the Literature.' *The Theological Educator,* March 2007 (2.1).

Nicholls, B. J. 'The Role of Spiritual Development in Theological Education.' *Evangelical Review of Theology* 19, no. 3 (1995): 231.

Shaw, I. *Best Practice Guidelines for Doctoral Programs.* Carlisle: Langham Global Library, 2015.

Warfield, B. B. *The Religious Life of Theological Students, Lecture given at Autumn Conference at Princeton Theological Seminary, October 4, 1911.* Republished. New Jersey: Presbyterian and Reformed, n.d.

11

Supervision and Developing a Research Culture

Doctoral students should only be accepted into an environment that provides support for learning about, and doing, research; where research is already taking place; and a research culture exists.[1]

I live in a fairly cool and wet part of the northern hemisphere. I enjoy growing plants, but many fail to thrive in the cold and damp, and even in the glass conservatory in my house they struggle. Yet, when I travel to parts of Africa and Asia I find these plants thriving with no artificial aid, simply because they are in their natural environment. Things thrive and grow where they are in the right context. The same is true for doctoral students.

The research doctorate has been universally acknowledged as,

i) the pinnacle of scholarship;

ii) an award guarded by the stewards of the discipline, with respected holders of PhDs acting as examiners;

iii) a research-orientated product produced by an individually responsible researcher, gaining specialized knowledge, which is set in the context of universal scholarship.

To be undertaken successfully, doctoral research must be undertaken in the appropriate context. The focus in educational thinking has tended to shift from the doctorate, to 'doctoral education,' – the broad framework within which doctoral studies take place. This emphasis on the activities and relationships that are required behind doing doctoral work has produced a much more healthy emphasis on the personal dimensions of doctoral studies. There is now greater recognition of the need for an understanding of the pedagogies, processes, and facilities required in training and supporting students needed in doctoral programs.

---

1. Shaw, *Best Practice*, Section 11.

The purpose of doctoral education is to produce the 'self-managing learner.'[2] This is a much bigger goal than helping someone to produce a single piece of research that gains a doctorate, but involves preparing a doctoral student for a lifetime of ministry in research and academic work. As well as involving a relationship between supervisor and student, it is also an experience in a public educational context. Achieving this takes a great deal more than the best efforts of the supervisor, although developing their professional skills in research and supervision is a vital component.

Developing a PhD program in an institution does not mean just adding another program to the institutional profile, or adding a higher level of teaching to what is on offer. Making an institution a suitable environment for research involves a significant change in the focus of its work, and a shift in its culture. It means asking fundamental questions about what the institution is for. This is a step that needs careful thought, significant investment, and the exercise of prayer and imagination.

As the ICETE *Best Practice Guidelines* state:

> *Doctoral programs should only be run where a research culture has been established, and where research is encouraged. This is the proper context for research-based learning.*[3]

1. Key Aspects of the Research Culture

The decision about whether to run a PhD program within an evangelical academic institution is a discussion about what type of institution it is going to be. This is a decision that needs the full support and endorsement of the wider academic community. Offering research doctoral programs is a statement that the institution is not just committed to doctoral students, but to producing research and advanced-level critical interaction. The institution is making a statement about its desire to be a place of serious, and leading edge, theological thinking and learning. This is a vital component of the environment in which research doctoral programs survive. It involves serious investment in due academic process and intellectual capital. Those who act as supervisors need to have the time and resources to supervise, they need to remain research-active, and to make their own contribution to cutting-edge academic discourse.

In some academic contexts, especially major universities, research is encouraged by generous research grants, and research time. However, in most evangelical institutions, the resources to support this are much more limited. Yet, a reduced supply of resources does not lessen its importance, and positive steps should be implemented to achieving this.

---

2. J. Stephenson, 'Managing Their Own Program,' *Studies in Continuing Education* 28, no. 1 (2006): 17–32.
3. Shaw, *Best Practice*, Section 17.

Doctoral research students are asked to develop original and creative responses to vital research questions. They need to be supervised by those who are research-active, have a good and current research record, who function well within their discipline, and who engage in peer-level dialogue at academic conferences and forums. They need to model what they expect of their research students. The institution where supervisors teach, and where doctoral students research, should be intentional about facilitating these opportunities, and making them available for their research students.

Reflective Questions

What does the term 'research culture' mean to you?

List three characteristics of a 'good' research culture.

Describe a situation in which you were involved where there was an 'enabling' research culture.

Describe a situation in which you were involved where there was a 'poor' research culture.

What can be done to develop a better research culture in your own institution?

---

2. Creating a Research Culture

Research thrives in supportive environments. This includes the presence of high quality postgraduate masters programs which include a research element, and develop research skills in future doctoral students (see chs. 4 and 5). The institutional context also needs to positively encourage thinking and research, such that this features as a key value in the institution's identity. This involves a commitment to facilitate academic faculty in research in their fields of expertise, and to maintain a fruitful ongoing dialogue with their academic peers. It feeds into the capacity to conduct personal research, supervise research students, but also permeates teaching at postgraduate masters level, and at undergraduate level.

A research culture is not just a place where research takes place. It is an aspect of a critically reflective learning culture, where the capacity to think fresh thoughts, and welcome creative insights, becomes a core value.

A research culture is an ideas culture. Fresh approaches and perspectives by students and supervisors are positively encouraged. They are seen as a vital resource for the wider church community, helping them to reflect on how to live and think in their own culture, and as a way of evangelical scholars contributing to global academic discourse.

The Research Seminar

The research seminar plays a key role in:

    i)   the development of a research culture,

    ii)   enhancing the wider research facilities available,

    iii)   supporting the training to doctoral research level of the student.

Doctoral students need an appropriate forum for the presentation of their ideas, or listening to those of their academic peers. The research seminar serves as a locus for peer-level academic debate, and facilitating discourse about cutting-edge thinking. It offers research students opportunity to gain experience of presenting their ideas, and learning the skills of conducting scholarly academic dialogue.

The seminar should provide opportunities for staff and students to engage in critical interaction with the ideas of visiting academics.

The research seminar can take a variety of formats – a single paper followed by discussion, or a series of short papers or reports on research in progress followed by discussion. Ideally papers should be distributed in advance to assist critical reflection, although often that does not prove feasible.

To run successfully it involves a commitment of time on the part of supervisors and students. It functions best when undertaken regularly – ideally at least once a month.

Here are some of the contributions it makes to the research culture:

    i)   It keeps supervisors fresh and stimulated toward regularly contributing to new thinking, and hence equipped for research and teaching.

    ii)   Because the topics are rarely exactly within the student's research field, the research seminar encourages supervisors and postgraduate students to think outside their immediate horizons, to think in interdisciplinary fashion. This can produce creative research approaches, and broader understandings.

    iii)   It provides a safe environment where postgraduates and supervisors can test out ideas, with peer evaluation and critique. These can be original research ideas, or questions arising from current academic discourse. The opportunity to do this in a formal setting, followed by respectful academic dialogue, helps to enhance the intellectual self-worth of the student.

    iv)   Opportunity should be taken to invite visiting scholars to deliver papers, which serves to expose the local academic community to fresh ideas and approaches from visiting scholars, and wider regional or global academic discourse.

v)   It helps academic faculty and students grow intellectually, relationally and spiritually around the core value of training creative Christian minds.

Running the Seminar

Flexibility and imaginative approaches should be attempted. The seminar needs to be properly moderated, and wide-ranging discussion fostered. If as a supervisor you take on the role of moderator it is important to ensure that research students are allowed to find their voice, and not sit silently while faculty members dominate the dialogue. Papers need to be intelligible to those present, and if interdisciplinary, they should be accessible to non-experts in specific fields, without losing their academic rigor.

Papers can be submitted in advance for review, briefly introduced, and then discussed, or presented in full at the seminar followed by questions and debate. Shorter papers of twenty minutes on research in progress can be developed.

Another fruitful approach is to take a key text – primary or secondary – which all members read, and a discussion around this follows. This can be within a specific research field, or may relate to educational developments.

To succeed, the seminar needs institutional ownership. Academic supervisors and postgraduate researchers need to commit to this for a couple of hours whenever it is held. It is a matter of courtesy and respect to attend and support those who are presenting papers. The research seminar helps to build mutual support, shared learning, and scholarly support and encouragement.

Reflective Questions

Does your institution run a research seminar?

How effective do you find it as a locus for peer-level academic debate?

What can you do to enhance its effectiveness?

How can you help your research students to get the most from the research seminar?

---

3. Building Library Resources

Despite the increasing availability of remote access to electronic study resources and databases, the library still serves as the 'heart' of the academic institution. Providing a proper environment in which research will thrive requires extensive investment in library resources. The supervisor needs to play a significant role in this through being actively involved in recommending key texts and resources for library purchase, and working to maintain the academic currency of the library in their research field. The library budget should be used creatively to support individual students in their need for high quality research resources. The position of librarian is essential to this, and should not just be seen as a minor administrative role, but as a core dimension of the teaching and research work of the institution. In the seminary where I taught, the librarian served on the academic board.

4. Creating Designated Study Facilities for Research Students

As students undertake research they need space for their books, notes, and research materials. It is frustrating to have to carry large numbers of books to a general study desk in the library, and remove them at the end of the day. A number of seminaries and universities have created designated postgraduate research study room for researchers, or a demarcated area in library. Others provide small designated offices, study cubicles or carrels. All these enhance the capacity of researchers to continue their work. If the provision is of a designated research room, this helps researchers have a sense of identity, and a mutually supportive research community can emerge.

5. Building Time for Supervision into Faculty Workloads

A number of institutions eager to introduce doctoral programs into their work then make no special provision of time for those involved in this. The institutions somehow expect it to be fitted in with everything else. Supervisory meetings take time, and so does reading and commenting on the work of research students, so failure to provide space in workloads is not good practice.

Quality Assurance considerations must ensure that the quality of supervision is not put at risk as a result of an excessive volume and range of responsibilities assigned to individual supervisors.

If asked to undertake the supervision of research students, it is important to ensure that you arrange with the leadership of your institution to build proper time allowance for supervisory meetings of postgraduates into your regular workload allocation. Your institution should have in place guidelines on the maximum number of research students (including those undertaking masters-level research) a supervisor can supervise at any one time. Academic and administrative workloads need to be adjusted to reflect supervision loads.

A reasonable estimate of the workload time it takes for a supervisor to supervise one full-time research doctoral student is 60–90 hours work per year.

This will vary somewhat, with more time required at the early stages of a student's program, and less in the second year. Experienced supervisors may find the time needed is slightly less. Establishing this time allowance should be part of your annual discussions as to workload with your head of department or Academic Dean. You should not overcommit yourself by accepting too many doctoral students for supervision. This will be harmful to your work, the student experience, and your overall health.

6. Professional Development of Supervisors

Many supervisors are asked to take on the role without any formal training or preparation to supervise. Yet, such is the importance of good supervision to successful research work that institutions offering doctoral degrees should put in place appropriate provisions for faculty development and training for supervisors of doctoral candidates. Reading this handbook is a start, and the ICETE Doctoral Committee also offers training seminars for supervisors, as do some local universities. It is important to emphasize how important this is to the leader of your doctoral program, and encourage that such facilities be made available regularly. Discussion seminars can be arranged around the contents of this handbook.

Work to ensure that institutional development plans include provisions for the identification and training of future academic supervisors. They need to be mentored in the work they will undertake. This may involve an element of your own time if you are an experienced supervisor and are asked to mentor others.

7. Maintaining Research Currency

Institutions offering doctoral degrees need to create structures to enable academic faculty engaged in doctoral supervision to maintain their research-level academic currency as part of their faculty development provisions.

This should result in doctoral supervisors regularly producing monographs, academic journal articles and papers in their subject area, and attendance and presentation of papers at academic conferences. If you have a heavy teaching or administrative load this is not easy, and urgent tasks push out the important research activity. Investment of your time in these research activities is essential to maintaining your fitness to supervise. Where this proves impossible, your academic currency will rapidly diminish and you should no longer continue to supervise.

The maintenance of such academic currency needs to be supported by the provision of study days and periods of sabbatical leave free of teaching and administration. It is important to discipline your time so that you can make full use of these, and not allow such provision to be taken up with other tasks. Active research feeds into good supervision, inspiring teaching, and the capacity to examine the work of others.

The institution needs to see that investment in its academic leadership requires investment in intellectual capital, and also the provision of opportunities for the growth in spiritual maturity of its academic leaders.

Reflective Questions

What major issues has this raised about these issues in your own institution?

What are the major areas that need attention in your own work?

Identify three key steps that need to be taken to address the areas identified for attention.

8. Conferences

It is important to maintain your own academic currency by attending, and wherever possible presenting papers at, academic conferences. These can be national, regional, and international. This allows you to engage with the most recent trends in scholarship, and network with your academic peers. Wherever possible you should present research work on these occasions – the need to prepare and deliver academic papers helps focus the mind on a research outcome.

In all this there is a cost. Institutions have limited resources. Staff development budgets are often the first to be cut, but this can speedily undermine the commitment of the institution to research-led teaching. Many conferences offer travel bursaries to those who attend, and full opportunity should be taken to benefit from these.

It is also possible for institutions to periodically host their own conferences on key themes. A few invited speakers can be supplemented by more local academics, and students whose research is at an advanced stage. The supervisor should do all they can to encourage development of such opportunities for the sake of their research students, the institution, and their own research profile.

Conferences can be arranged at a local level for the benefit of local church leaders and pastors, helping them to understand scholarly perspectives on issues in their local contexts. This helps with a commitment to promote lifelong learning among church leaders, and enables the seminary to serve the local church and promote thinking on contextual needs and issues.

9. Publications

Research-led universities not only encourage but also reward research publication activity. Research activity is usually rated according to an external reference measurement to determine its relative standing within the community of peer-reviewed journals. In some contexts additional payment is received for research publications.

In the evangelical theological institution, the resources for this may be more limited, but the ethos should be the same. Good research should be shared, discussed, and disseminated widely. The overall readership for academic papers and peer-reviewed monographs may not be large, but they are usually read by the key players in the academic debate. Therefore, having a strategic input into shaping the trajectory of scholarship is a very important activity. To bring a distinctive evangelical perspective into such academic discourse is an aspect of Christian mission. There is also need to write and publish materials that will benefit students and church leaders. This connects the academy with the church, and helps it to serve the wider work and witness of those churches.

Research students should be encouraged to publish their research work, not only as a research monograph, but articles can also be developed from chapters in their thesis, or which are related to their research. Other versions can be produced that serve the needs of church leaders in the context.

Summary

The doctoral degree should not exist in isolation, but should be integrated into the work of the whole institution. Students should not feel isolated from other students and the wider community.

Research supervisors need to play a full part in the research culture, and in promoting it across the institution. They should do this on the conviction that:

i)   Research feeds good teaching – there is a strong synergy between the two.

ii) Good research ideas percolate through the academic community, and raise the quality of thinking and academic discourse among colleagues.

iii) Engaging with academic discourse at peer level from an evangelical perspective is an aspect of Christian mission.

iv) Other programs will benefit from the resources developed and the academic interchange encouraged.

v)   The contribution to an institution of a well-developed research culture cannot be measured simply in financial terms – but should be seen as a way of bringing further depth, maturity, and richness to the task of training Christian leaders and thinkers for the context.

Reflective Questions

To what degree did the research culture where you undertook your doctoral research enhance your research experience?

What could have been done to improve this?

What sort of research culture exists in the context where you currently teach?

List the activities that you undertake that contribute to the research culture where you teach currently.

What ideas do you have to further build the research culture in your own institution?

If your institution is just starting to build a research culture, and has limited funds, where would you start?

How can you help your students to contribute to, and benefit from, the research culture?

Case Study

At Paolo's seminary, where he leads the research program, a research seminar has been introduced. The first seminars go well, but Paolo notices that the academic faculty tend to dominate the debate, and research students contribute very little. After one paper the discussion becomes very heated, and there is a strong exchange of views between two faculty members, which leaves the students present feeling uncomfortable. When Paolo discusses this with the faculty members they both say it is impossible to argue for a particular position without being passionate about it. He is fearful that emotions are clouding the arguments.

Questions

What issues does this raise?

What should Paolo do to help improve the atmosphere at the seminar, and model good academic practice?

Further Reading

Eley, A., and R. Murray. *How to Be an Effective Supervisor*. Maidenhead: Open University Press, 2009.

Quality Assurance Agency, 'Doctoral Degree Characteristics.' www.qaa.ac.uk/en/Publications/Documents/Doctoral_Characteristics. pdf

Shaw, I. *Best Practice Guidelines for Doctoral Programs*. Carlisle: Langham Global Library, 2015.

12

Keeping Doctoral Students Writing

I write, I write again, I write a third time . . . then I take the third – I literally
fill the page with corrections so that another person could not read it – then I
write it out fair for the printer. Then I put it by – I take it up again – I begin to
correct again – it will not do – alterations multiply – pages are rewritten – little
lines sneak in and crawl about – the whole page is disfigured – I write again.
I cannot tell how many times this process has gone on. I can but compare the
whole business to a very homely undertaking – washing a sponge of the sea
gravel and sea smell.[1]

So wrote John Henry Newman, one of England's most famous nineteenth-century
theologians. If he found the process of writing, putting the right words in the right
order, so difficult, it is no surprise that our doctoral students also do!

The Challenge of Writing

Few doctoral students enter doctoral programs as fully formed, highly confident, and
capable writers. Academic writing is a skill that needs to be honed and developed
throughout the process of doctoral studies. Because the final examination in the
doctorate centers upon the written assessment of a thesis, writing skills are essential.
Doctoral students need to start writing early. The old model of a doctoral student sitting
and reading for several years, and then 'writing up' a thesis in the final few months, is
now recognized to be unsatisfactory. Indeed failure to write regularly, and keep deadlines
for submissions of pieces of work, is a marker of problems with the student's approach.
Studies have identified difficulties in starting to write as a frequent reason for failure to

---

1. J. H. Newman, *Letters and Diaries of John Henry Newman*, Vol. VI (Oxford: Clarendon Press, 1961),
188–189.

submit a thesis, or for submitting a thesis that requires extensive revision and correction.[2] Therefore, there is a vital need to integrate the teaching of the scholarly writing process into the initial stage of doctoral study.

Writing is different from public speaking or preaching, although there are similarities. The speaker will receive immediate feedback, and can deal with questions or issues of lack of clarity quickly. Material can be added, changed or corrected, based on the reaction of the audience. In writing, feedback to authors is more remote, and takes longer to receive – book reviews can come out several years after a book is published. The written form is more set, and open to judgment in a different way to how speaking is assessed. Responses to writing can be more formal, less personal, and because they cannot be explained and nuanced in a way verbal responses are, they can appear colder and even harsher.

The term 'Writing Up' can sound rather casual, implying that the research is largely done and all that is left is quickly putting together a few chapters to complete the thesis. Instead writing up is hard. It involves concentrated and profound thinking. It requires the writer to express complex thoughts logically and lucidly on paper. It demands that the writer substantiates in writing the claims of the thesis.

Getting onto paper what you understand in your head is not easy. Some students can see an issue conceptually, and maybe can explain it verbally, but when it comes to writing, words fail them.

Writing is making meaning through language. It is part of a process of negotiation between the writer and the members of the discourse community for whom he or she is writing. Everything a doctoral student writes will be closely examined at the end of the process. It must stand up to rigorous scrutiny – does it make sense, is it understandable to others? It needs to be carefully thought over and reassessed. Students need to learn to interrogate what they write to ensure that it conveys what their intention is, because others will read, interpret and make meaning of what they have written. They must weigh whether each sentence is informative, with appropriate and relevant information, and without 'waffle.' Are all the arguments and pieces of evidence substantiated? It is unlikely the student will be able to produce the finished product at the first attempt. Several drafts allow a piece of work to mature and be honed, with several chances to sort out problems, rather than rushed together at the last minute. We hope that the process is not as tortuous as John Henry Newman found it, but it might be so!

---

2. E. Rudd, *A New Look at Postgraduate Failure* (Guildford, Surrey: Society for Research into Higher Education, 1985).

Barriers to Writing

Writers are famously prone to procrastination. Writing is not a 'natural' process in the way that speaking is. Its skills need to be learned and constantly developed. Many writers are plagued by a sense of failure about their work. Even well-known novelists will talk about how hard it is to face a blank piece of paper, or a blank screen at the start of the day. They will also speak about 'writer's block,' a time when the words simply will not come. Writing is an individual, and can be an isolating, activity.

Reflective Questions

Reflect on your own feelings about writing.

What have been the major challenges you have faced?

What has been the most successful writing you have undertaken?

What lay behind making it successful?

The Importance of Getting Students to Write Small Sections Regularly

Getting students to regularly write up sections of work is important for a number of reasons:

i)   It enables them to reflect on where they have got in their thinking, and where they are going. This creates summative moments in a formative process.

ii)   The act of writing can be a powerful way of generating ideas and recalling information.

iii) Discussing a written piece of work that will eventually form part of the thesis / dissertation allows for feedback to be given. Although not formally graded, the supervisor can see and comment on the standard of the student's work, and offer correction and direction.

iv)   The production of assessed pieces of work is usually an institutional requirement for progression reviews, upgrades, etc.

Why are students reluctant to submit work? There are various causes:

i)   A thesis is always in a process of 'coming into being'. Students feel that the product is not finished, so they are reluctant to submit what seems like half-finished work.

ii)   Students feel that their skills are not well developed so they are reluctant to show work to their supervisors.

iii) Students have not been trained how to write long pieces of work in their previous studies.

iv)   They are haunted by a fear of failure, or being 'judged' prematurely.

Reflective Questions

What were the reasons you have had personally for being reluctant to write?

What tasks did your supervisors set to start you writing?

What approaches have you taken to get your students writing?

Particular Barriers to Writing

Difficulty in writing is not simply due to academic failings or weakness. If students are having difficulty writing, the supervisor should explore what might lie behind this.

Stress: Writing a thesis is very stressful. As the pressures of deadlines and the enormity of the task mount, some students find the ability to write diminishes. Some students experience severe headaches. Others may spend much time staring blankly at the screen. If this becomes extreme, some students may need to be referred for medical assistance, for symptoms linked to severe stress or depression.

Lack of organization: Some students are unable to settle on a time and a place to write. Maybe their notes are not in an orderly or accessible fashion. It takes great personal and mental discipline to get all the required elements for sustained writing in place at the right time.

Too many distractions: Writing takes deep concentration, and with constant interruptions from email, texts, telephone calls, or family or pastoral demands students find it hard to focus their thoughts. Faced by these pressures there is a need to get away to a quiet place to write in concentrated fashion.

Failure to give writing priority: Many students find the original research, extending the boundaries of a subject area, exciting and stimulating. Writing, in comparison, can appear dull. However, the 'reporting back' phase of research is as important as evidence gathering itself.

Some learning disability: It is possible that some students have reached doctoral stage with an undiagnosed learning disability, such as dyslexia. The greater the challenge of vast quantities of reading, and then writing long, concentrated, intensely thought out pieces of work, the more an underlying issue can be highlighted. If serious difficulties become apparent, it might be necessary to refer a student for professional assessment to see if there is a cause, and advice given on appropriate strategies to deal with this. Those who have such disabilities should not be discouraged from attempting doctoral-level work – I have supervised students with dyslexia to success at masters and doctoral level. With appropriate specialist support students facing these issues can succeed.

Understanding and Teaching the Writing Process

Writing involves deploying the skills of planning, building content, understanding process, and offering critique.

Planning

The importance of spending time in producing an initial outline plan of a piece of work should be emphasized to doctoral students. Some supervisors request to see these before each stage of the writing begins. The outline plan is the skeleton of the chapter or section, and the evidence and argumentation is the flesh that is added on to this.

The plan should establish the structure of the essay, and demonstrate the clarity of the argument being made. The main points of the section plan become the headings and subheadings in the essay.

In producing the plan, some students find it helpful to use pre-writing strategies such as brainstorming and mind mapping in order to generate and organize their ideas before starting the section.

The First Draft

After planning, writing begins. It is good for students to be able to write concertedly at the initial stage, letting their ideas flow, without spending a long time polishing the technical aspects which can interrupt the generation of ideas. A first draft should be left for about a day before it is revised.

Revision

The student should carefully read over the draft, looking for points of repetition, lack of clarity, or inaccuracy. After these corrections a further period of time should be spent checking style, grammar and spelling.

Sentences should be of appropriate length. Where they are long and rambling, this needs to be pointed out and addressed. Sometimes they are so short it is hard to follow an argument. A variety in length and form is generally more interesting.

Technical apparatus such as footnotes should then be corrected.

The student should at an early stage adopt the approach of one of the academic style guides (such as the *Chicago Manual of Style*[3]), and consistently stick to it. The supervisor should make recommendations as to the style guides acceptable in the institution.

Even with early drafts, high standards of writing and presentation should be insisted on. Key skills for the future are being learned and consolidated.

The Writing Style

The style should be appropriate for the level and the subject matter. Supervisors need to give regular advice as to the 'language of discourse' – and the proper use of subject-specific technical language. However, even when technical language is used, the prose should not become inaccessible, or dull.

Logical Flow

Chapters and sections should have an introduction, which serves as a signpost to what will follow. If there are subsections, the major ones should be indicated here. The introduction should draw the reader in, arousing interest, even a little intrigue. A thought provoking quotation, or another scholar's argument, can serve as a way of drawing the reader in. Even in the introduction, the conclusion needs to be kept in mind – where this is all leading.

The Overall Argument

A thesis should have an overarching argument – a meta-narrative. So too should the individual chapters.

A good exercise when assessing the logical flow of a piece of work is to read the introduction, and then go to the conclusion, without initially looking at what is in between, and see if there is a connection between the start and end of the piece – are the questions posed in the introduction, or issues raised, subsequently answered?

Structure

Within the thesis, each section should have a clear structure – with a brief introduction, appropriate subject matter and argumentation, and conclusion summing up where the argument has reached. This then serves as a bridge into the next key stage of the argument.

---

3. *The Chicago Manual of Style* (16th Edition, University of Chicago, Chicago, 2010).

The Main Content

The main body of the chapter or section needs to concentrate on substantiating the key argument, or body of evidence. The focus here is on *describing* and *explaining*.

The student needs to create a sense of scholarly debate and academic discourse, which they understand and arbitrate on. This involves employing the skills of the critical discourse in the subject area, with arguments for one side and another. A dialectic approach is common – ideally the student's work builds from thesis to antithesis into synthesis, and on to new thesis – new paradigms of understanding.

The importance of using words like *although, however, in contrast, moreover, furthermore, finally, on the one hand . . . on the other hand* should be stressed as ways of building an academic argument. Terms such as *therefore, thus, it follows that, so, hence* are important tools in the concluding sections of chapters and the whole thesis.

The Conclusion

The conclusion is the culmination of the preceding argument – emphasizing the most important parts, acknowledging weaker areas, and asserting the 'thesis' that has been presented in sustained form. It often contains ideas for further work that is needed on the subject that the student or others may undertake later.

The Critical Friend

Students are usually encouraged to have pieces read by a critical friend who can 'see' the mistakes the writer often misses. However, the ground rules in this need to be made clear. The 'critical friend' should not go beyond highlighting issues in presentation, style and grammar, and must not 'improve' the student's work in other ways. A good spelling and style checker in a word processing package should eliminate many of these issues. If students are not working in their first language, good levels of support in this area are important.

Final Presentation

Students need to learn the importance of high standards of presentation in writing a thesis. From the outset they should be given instructions on appropriate font size, word spacing, margins, etc. Double line spacing makes it easier for the supervisor to review the work.

Tables, figures, lists of references or appendices should all be attached and numbered sequentially.

Academic writing must be precise and clear. There can be no room for misinterpretation or misunderstanding. At a thesis defense, a student should not find themselves saying, 'What I really meant was . . .'.

Reflective Questions

How can you best encourage your doctoral students in these skills?

What style manual do you use, and recommend?

What examples of academic writing can you use to demonstrate these skills?

How do you assess the readability and understandability of a text?

Helping to Create Structure and Meaning – Some Clear Checkpoints for the Supervisor

i)   Has the student made the intention of each section or chapter clear?

ii)   Is the argument / analysis clear?

iii)   Has the student respected the writing conventions of the discipline?

iv)   Have the points made been supported by evidence?

v)   Are the conclusions highlighted and explicit?

vi)   Have links between this and other work been made clear?

Reflective Questions

Which writing strategies have worked with your students?

Which have not?

What ideas or techniques do you recommend for getting writing started as the day begins?

When there is need for a major stimulus to progress their writing more quickly:

　　　Can the student change their mode of working?

　　　Can they go up a gear and increase output?

It can be useful to share with students your own writing strategies, and the ups and downs of your writing progress. Some writers recommend that the way to get writing restarted at the beginning of the day is to leave an unfinished sentence on the page you are working on. The first task is to complete the sentence at the start of the next day – and so writing is resumed.

Creating Closure

'Closure' is bringing to an end an aspect of the research. It means 'limiting, enclosing, shutting down'. It does not necessarily mean a piece of work has reached its final form, but it is at the stage at which it can be left for now, and revisited later. Writing is creating a series of little closures. At these points, students can select, prioritize, and filter out ideas they are not going to develop.

Reflective Questions

What points of closure has the student reached in what they have done?

What points of closure do they need to reach now?

The Accountability Partner – The Research Journal

This is recommended in many of the manuals about thesis writing. Some doctoral programs make this a requirement as part of the personal development profile of their students. In this the student records:

i) Progress made, meetings held, what the student did and when they did it.

ii) It is important for students to calibrate their progress – to adjust writing or thinking according to how they are getting along.

iii) Reflections on their thinking so far, ideas that are developing. It should include space for brainstorming, jotting down key new ideas as they develop. In the journal the student should write down major problems foreseen, and the 'eureka' type moments when the resolutions become clearer.

iv) Refocus – what is left to do, when and where will it be done?

v) Plan ahead – students tend to have an unrealistic assessment of how long it will take to write a well-developed piece of academic work. Get students to work out how long it takes them to write 500 words of well-developed academic text. Then ask them to draw up a rough writing plan for the next year based on their track record of speed of writing.

The Postgraduate Writing Course

Short-term writing courses can be helpful for developing academic writing skills. The most helpful ones focus on the production of text, and not solely on the sorting out of ideas prior to putting pen to paper. They involve input from experts in academic writing, and develop ways in which students can critique each others' work.[4]

Reflective Questions

During your own doctoral studies, did you attend a writing course? Was it helpful?

What postgraduate writing support courses does your institution offer?

If such a course is offered, what key elements should it contain?

If a course is not available, what self-help books on thesis writing can you recommend?

Offering Feedback as Part of the Training Process

In a study of forty-five doctoral students it was found that preparing and receiving critiques from professors and peers was perceived to be the *'most influential element in helping them to understand the process of scholarly writing and in producing a better written product.'* In building their confidence as academic writers *'personalized face-to-face feedback; and the iterative or ongoing nature of the critiques they received'* was essential. Yet, the students also recognized that the critiquing process was *'highly emotional and at times frustrating'*. The study concluded that it is vital to assist students in learning how to both receive and give useful feedback.[5]

This means that feedback from supervisors is very important in the process of academic formation. How it is done needs to be thought through carefully. Supervisors need to develop ways to help students to receive and benefit from feedback – whether from supervisor, peers in an academic seminar, or from external academic reviewers.

---

4. M. S. Torrance and G. V. Thomas, 'The Development of Writing Skills in Doctoral Research Students,' in *Postgraduate Education and Training in the Social Sciences. Processes and Products*, ed. R. G. Burgess (London: Jessica Kingsley, 1994), 105–123.

5. R. S. Caffarella and B. G. Barnett, 'Teaching Doctoral Students to Become Scholarly Writers: The Importance of Giving and Receiving Critiques,' *Studies in Higher Education* 25, no. 1 (2000): 40–43.

Reflective Questions

What sort of feedback do you offer to your students – written, oral, in advance, on the day?

How long does it take after submission of a piece of work before feedback is offered?

How is negative feedback delivered?

Styles of Giving Feedback

Feedback allows students to understand the standards they must meet to gain a PhD, and measure whether that are meeting those standards or not. This is important, because students have few opportunities to measure how they are doing.

I was struck many years ago by comments from one of my research students. They had submitted a long, and on the whole good, piece of work, which I commented on substantially and largely positively with many encouragements. But the student's response was that because I had written the comments in red ink, it looked like the feedback was all negative. It was a simple, but important, lesson to learn. Ask yourself, what unintended messages are you conveying as you give feedback in different forms?

Writing is a very personal act – it is thinking your thoughts out loud in semi-permanent form. Therefore, the feelings of self-worth of students as researchers and writers are closely tied to this process of having their work publicly critiqued. Moments of critical feedback can be difficult emotionally for writers. They can raise profound questions about their ability to write, and even whether they should continue in a doctoral program.

Here are two descriptions from students given in published studies about receiving feedback:

> *'My first response, if they have a lot of suggestions, should be profound relief that I have someone in my life who will be honest with me and help me do the very best work of which I am capable. But my first thought is, 'Well, I'm sorry, but I can't be friends with you anymore, because you must have a bad personality to write about my work in this way. And a bad character.'*
>
> *'Sometimes I can't get words to come out of my mouth because I am so disappointed.'*

Reflective Questions

How did you feel when something you wrote received a bad review?

How would you have given that feedback differently?

How do you want students to respond to your feedback?

What would you do if they challenged your comments?

Managing Feedback Sessions

It is important to manage the supervisory relationship at the key moments when feedback is being given. All that most students intuitively know is that they should try to be non-defensive when receiving feedback and learn to receive negative feedback with grace.

- As a supervisor, think through the feedback process before you start to give it. What is it intended to achieve, and how do you want your student to react?
- In their initial orientation with students, the supervisor should give in-depth direction about how they will give feedback, and how it should be received. This will need to be reinforced at various points.
- Students need to learn how to handle conflicting feedback from different supervisors. As far as possible, these conflicts should be resolved between the supervisors before they meet the student, and not played out in front of the student, otherwise they will find this confusing and distressing.
- Supervisors should carefully consider what the critiquing process is intended to achieve and prepare materials for students which will help them incorporate this process into their learning practice as students.
- Acknowledge that being critiqued is both a rational and an emotional process for most people. Research students are judged on what they write. The stakes are high and students are deeply invested emotionally in their work.
- Try to convey a sense of achievement – feedback needs to show what has been achieved, in addition to what needs to be improved. It is not enough just to say 'write better'. It is better to say, 'this is what you have done well and this is how you can write better . . .'
- In the process of giving feedback on academic work, it is important to teach students to be critically reflective of their own work. When they move into future ministry as teachers, scholars, and writers, they will need to exercise their own independent professional judgment. This is a skill they have to steadily learn. Students will learn this from being critiqued, and critiquing the work of others. Doing this in a supportive environment is most helpful.

Case Study

Noah has presented a piece of work filled with unclear expressions, spelling mistakes, and grammatical imprecision. The work needs extensive revision, but the deadline for submission is close, and as his supervisor you know that asking for the corrections will take a long time. You are thinking about going through the work and highlighting all the problems yourself, although you know it will take time. But you know that doing this will help ensure Noah gets the work in on time.

Questions

What you should do?

What should you not do?

Further Reading

Caffarella, R. S., and B. G. Barnett. 'Teaching Doctoral Students to Become Scholarly Writers: The Importance of Giving and Receiving Critiques.' *Studies in Higher Education* 25, no. 1 (2000): 39–52.

Chicago University Press. *A Manual for Writers of Term Papers, Theses and Dissertations* (7th edition). Chicago: Chicago University Press, 2010.

Cutts, Martin. *Oxford Guide to Plain English*. Oxford: Oxford University Press, 2009.

Kamler, B., and P. Thomson. *Helping Doctoral Students Write: Pedagogies for Supervision*. Abingdon: Routledge, 2006.

Murray, R. *How to Write a Thesis,* 2nd edition. Maidenhead: Open University Press, 2006.

Seely, J. *Oxford Guide to Effective Writing and Speaking*. Oxford: Oxford University Press, 2005.

Swan, Michael. *Practical English Usage*. Oxford: OUP, 1996, for English as foreign language, EFL.

Torrance, M., and G. Thomas. 'The Development of Writing Skills in Doctoral Research Students.' In *Postgraduate Education and Training in the Social Sciences. Processes and Products*, edited by R. G. Burgess, 105–123. London: Jessica Kingsley, 1994.

Torrance, M., G. Thomas, and E. Robinson. 'The Writing Experiences of Social Science Research Students.' *Studies in Higher Education* 17 (1992): 155–167.

———. 'Training in Thesis Writing: An Evaluation of Three Conceptual Orientations.' *British Journal of Educational Psychology* 63 (February 1993): 170–184.

13

Sustaining the Doctoral Process Administratively

Good supervision and facilities can all too easily be undermined by inadequacies in the finance office, or registration or administration processes. Complexities and delays in these areas can hamper the research progress of students, and significantly detract from the study experience of students. Excellence should be reflected at all levels and dimensions of the institution.[1]

Doctoral programs need well-functioning financial and administrative processes. Yet, there are very few academic colleagues that I know who really like administration, although some are good at it and have a very special gifting in this area. Most see it as a chore, and others as a matter which takes low priority. It seems to get in the way of the 'real' academic life – which is teaching, researching, writing, and engaging personally with students. Yet, it is vital to good academic process to maintain records, write reports, ensure timely completion of forms, and attend meetings. I am regularly involved in supporting doctoral students who encounter very great frustration because supervisors do not complete forms, or write necessary reports. It can delay their progression, their examinations, and their completion times. It can mean vital resources of time and finance are used up while they wait for due process to be completed. I have known students left waiting months for the official results of examinations or resubmissions simply because someone has failed to complete a form or report, or a meeting has not been convened. This is deeply stressful and unfair to students. It can cause major problems with funding and sponsoring agencies, and could potentially lead to funding being withheld or denied.

Excellence needs to be the hallmark of doctoral supervision, and attention to the detail in process is part of this. It helps ensure the experience is good for the student as well as the supervisor.

---

1. Shaw, *Best Practice*, Section 14.

This Issue Has Spiritual Dimensions

The Apostle Paul expresses this well in Colossians 3:23 – 'Whatever you do, work at it with all your heart, as working for the Lord, not for human masters.' We should remember that faithful work even in these routine tasks done for the Lord is a dimension of worship. As the Christian poet George Herbert expressed it in the seventeenth century:

> Teach me, my God and King,
>   In all things thee to see,
> And what I do in any thing,
>   To do it as for thee:

> A servant with this clause
>   Makes drudgerie divine:
> Who sweeps a room, as for thy laws,
>   Makes that and th' action fine.

To many academics, administration, completing forms, compiling reports, attending requirement meetings is as big a 'drudgerie' as sweeping a room. Yet, as faithful service offered to the Lord, it is one dimension of leading our lives as acts of living sacrifice.

So too, in the famous hymn *'Fill thou my life, O Lord my God, in every part with praise'* written by Horatius Bonar in 1866, praise is brought into all aspects and circumstances of life – as he puts it in the third verse –

> Praise in the common things of life,
> its goings out and in;
> praise in each duty and each deed,
> however small and mean.

We should do all things, including small, routine, administrative tasks, as unto the Lord.

The Importance of Quality Assurance

Across the world programs are everywhere battling against grade inflation (or deflation), and also credentialing inflation. Supervisors need to play their role in ensuring a PhD is a PhD wherever it is delivered.

This means that quality assurance mechanisms for the delivery and measurement of the level and success of PhD programs need to be in place.

Supervisors need to consider how, in striving for excellence, the provisions and effectiveness of programs are measured. They must play a key role in ensuring that institutions monitor the success of their postgraduate research programs against appropriate internal and/or external indicators and targets. Where this is not happening, they must work to put in place systems to enable it to do so.

Ensuring Academic Standards Are Defined and Maintained

Institutions offering research degree programs must have ways of defining what the academic standards of their doctoral programs are. These criteria and procedures used to assess research degrees must be made clear to both students, supervisors, and external examiners. The achievements of graduates within doctoral courses need to be recorded. The quality of the work of doctoral students needs also to be assessed against external standards, especially the quality of work of doctoral students on other programs.

Reflective Questions

As a doctoral supervisor, rank out of ten how helpful you think the following options would be in ensuring that quality assurance and external benchmarking takes place:

i)   being part of supervisory teams in other institutions,

ii)   external examining,

iii)   inviting external examiners to examine your students' theses,

iv)   reading doctoral theses written by students in other contexts.

What issues and your personal practice arise from this?

Assessment Procedures, Regulations, Codes of Conduct

These will be drawn up by the appropriate academic boards, or postgraduate studies committees, and implemented by the leader of the research program. However, the individual supervisor must play an active role in their application and maintenance.

Assessment procedures need to be clear, and operated rigorously, fairly, and consistently by all in the institution. Regulations will be supplemented by similarly accessible, subject-specific guidance at the level of the faculty, school or department.

There should be clear codes of conduct and practice applicable across the institution relating to student and staff behavior, available to all students and staff involved in postgraduate research programs. These need to be implemented and regularly kept under review.

It is the responsibility of the program to ensure that the student receives copies of these regulations and codes of conduct and practice each year, and that students understand them. Supervisors should also each year reread and familiarize themselves with the regulations and guidance each year, so that they are in a position to answer student questions and offer advice.

Reflective Questions

When did you last reread your institution's regulations?

What sort of guidance are you most commonly asked for by doctoral students?

Who are the key people in your institution in providing the information students need?

Accreditation / Validation Issues

Most doctoral programs work with accreditation agencies or validators. By this means organizations outside the institution are involved in bringing external scrutiny and ensuring internationally accepted standards. The aim is to achieve academic equivalence across programs, even if delivery styles are different, to ensure the doctoral degree is credible, acceptable, and transferable across international academic contexts. Although as a supervisor you may not be involved directly in these matters, part of what is being regularly reported on and assessed is your performance as a supervisor, and the reports you write and the student support you offer are a vital part of this process. It is therefore important, for the sake of the institution as well as your students, to contribute to this process efficiently and wholeheartedly.

Reflective Questions

How does the institution assure the quality of the doctoral program offered?

What external measurements are used?

When problems arise, what is the agreed mechanism for addressing and resolving them?

Maintaining the Academic Process

Even if not holding a leadership or administrative position within the institution, there will be points at which you relate to the formal academic process within the institution, usually through a committee, or through relating to a line manager who oversees the doctoral programs. It is important that you and your students have a good understanding of this process, and where your role fits in. You and your students need to know where the primary locus for academic decision making lies in your institution where it relates to doctoral studies.

Reflective Questions

Who is your line manager when it relates to issues within the doctoral program, or academic or student-welfare issues?

How is this structure communicated to students?

What student representation is included in this structure?

To what degree are research students and staff empowered by this process, and if change is needed, where would you most like to see that take place?

Monitoring Student Progress

The institution needs clearly defined mechanisms for monitoring and supporting student progress, and these need to be communicated to students and relevant staff. The doctoral supervisor needs to have up-to-date familiarity the nature of these institutional processes for monitoring progression. As the main contact point with them, the supervisor should regularly raise issues relating to them with the student.

Two concerns that have been raised in doctoral education in a number of countries relate to student progress and student attrition. In too many cases, students spend far too long working on the dissertation, delaying graduation well beyond what was originally anticipated. Related to this is the concern over how many students enter the dissertation phase of their studies and do not complete their degrees. One of the challenges facing doctoral program directors, and dissertation committee chairs, is how to encourage students to keep their research projects moving, keeping the momentum up and not letting the research and writing stall out. One of the best ways to accomplish this is to have the student schedule regular times for interaction. Supervisors should ask students to be in contact with them every two weeks with a brief update, even if nothing of substance was accomplished in that time. Regular conversation keeps students from becoming isolated in their work, and can help get things moving again if they have come to a standstill. Frequent interaction allows you to monitor your student's progress and determine if there are obstacles that need to be overcome.

Reporting by Supervisors

During the research stage of their programs, doctoral students can often feel uncertain about how much progress they are making, which can create insecurity and frustration. They will have come from earlier levels of academic work where assignments are set, delivered to deadlines, and grades received. To submit pieces of work that receive detailed comments, but no grade (as is usual in doctoral work), is a new experience for students.

To assist students in their progression through a program, institutions must have in place a series of formal progress reviews at different stages. This ensures realistic expectations and appropriate standards are established, and provide a structure for the student's work. These reviews will involve the participation of both supervisors and students. Guidance should be provided to students, supervisors and others involved in monitoring progress reviews. It is important to maintain detailed records of the outcomes of these reviews. If a student is not working to an appropriate level, or progressing sufficiently well, they need to be made aware of this, so that they can make the necessary adjustments,

Playing an active role in this area is a very important part of supervising a student on a doctoral program, although it involves filling in forms or completing reports. Many supervisors give this a low priority, and need to be reminded repeatedly of the need to complete them, and not leave them unattended in the inbox. This is not fair to the student, or the head of the program or to student sponsoring organizations.

The completion of forms should not be simply a 'box-ticking exercise', but should provide a proper formal record of progress, achievements, and concerns. In most cases they will be a celebration of achievement, but in others they will prove a clear 'paper trail' of concerns being expressed, solutions proposed, and opportunities for remedy supplied. This is important if, in the end, there is not a successful outcome for the student.

Formal Reviews

The progress of doctoral students should normally be monitored formally at least once every six months, and annually for part-time students. These formal reviews should take place at key points in the progression of students, when key decisions about continuance in a doctoral program, and progression to the next stage, are needed. Student and academic faculty need to be prepared for when these reviews will take place.

Record Keeping

This is a vital part of sustaining the doctoral process. Students and supervisors should maintain good records of meetings held, issues discussed, guidance given, and work submitted. Samples of work should be retained. Guidance on how these records are to be kept and maintained should be given to students, supervisors and others involved in progress monitoring and review processes.

These records should relate to personal progress, and record the development of research and attainment of other skills.

Monitoring the Responsiveness of the Supervisory Team / Committee

Sometimes it is not students, but supervisors or doctoral committee members who do not keep up with the expected schedule for their review work. If you are the Supervisor / Chair of the dissertation committee, and your students find themselves waiting for overdue responses from committee members, encourage them to let you know if they are experiencing a pattern of delays so you can make enquiries and see if there is a way to get the review process moving forward. If you see that you have readers on your committee who need gentle reminders to keep up with their work, don't leave this to the student to address. Step in and find a way as a colleague to discuss the situation.

Reflective Questions

What regular records of meetings with students do you keep, and how are these submitted to the institution?

What reports to progression review boards, and external agencies, do you complete?

What are the review stages in your doctoral program?

What records of these review stages are kept?

What are the most frequent problems with getting responses from members of your doctoral committee?

Student Feedback

> Institutions offering doctoral programs must have in place appropriate mechanisms for dealing with formal and informal expressions of student feedback about supervision, including official complaints mechanisms. For disputes that cannot be resolved there should be provision for appeal to a final Third Party who is neutral and external to the institution, and who understands academic process.[2]

---

2. Shaw, *Best Practice*, Section 16.

Institutions offering doctoral programs need to collect, review and, where appropriate, respond to feedback from all concerned with postgraduate research programs. Students need to be confident that feedback that they give will be acted on. All procedures relating to feedback need to be fair, clear to all concerned, and applied consistently. Students should know that their feedback is valued, and taken seriously. They should receive information about the responses that have been made to their feedback, and actions taken.

It is easy for programs to assume everything is progressing well if there are no major complaints or evidence of student discontent. However, there can be significant issues that lie unresolved, or problems within the program that faculty need to be aware of. Action needs to be taken to prevent them harming the academic or leadership development of the students.

Doctoral programs should have a formal system for gaining feedback from students about their experience on the program, at least every twelve months and preferably every six months. This can be by means of a questionnaire, although it is possible to do this orally in a meeting with an independent third party. Ideally, the two approaches should be taken, allowing for quantitative analysis of responses, as well are more open ended and discursive comments to be received. Issues covered should include – quality of the research experience, facilities available (including library, computing and technology support), satisfaction with supervision, participation in research culture, community life, pastoral care and spiritual formation, etc. These feedback forms tend to be filled in anonymously. They allow students to identify issues arising. In the institution where I taught, each doctoral student had a meeting with an external Third Party, who held a senior position as Dean of Humanities in a local major research university, and was an evangelical Christian. Students found both mechanisms helpful, and the person-to-person interviews allowed issues to be raised informally that went beyond what was on the feedback form.

Within these reviews, there should be scope for feedback from students as to the quality of supervision they have received. In terms of developing supervision style, this feedback is helpful, and as reflective practitioners, supervisors should welcome this opportunity to learn and develop their own practice.

It is not always easy to be 'assessed' by your students in this way. However, in striving for excellence, we sometimes learn best when things are going less well, or criticisms are made. Supervisors should discuss issues raised with other academic leaders to see what actions should be taken, approaches changed, or maintained. Sample Annual and End of Program feedback forms are included as appendices 1 and 2.

Reflective Questions

How do you react to student feedback?

What key things have you learned and changed as a result of student feedback?

Reports from External Sources

Regular reports will be received from validators, accreditation agencies, and external examiners. These need to be read carefully by supervisors, as well as those who lead the program. Supervisors should play a full role in developing any responses that are made to this feedback. In this way doctoral supervisors need to engage actively in making the institution a self-reflective learning and growing community.

Student Representation

It is best practice to have formal student representation on the degree committees that deal with doctoral-level studies. Students should elect their representative, and he or she should meet and communicate with other students regularly. They become the formal channel for raising student concerns, and are a vital resource in ascertaining the student viewpoint on issues within the program, and possible enhancements or changes. As supervisor, it is important to encourage your students who you think are suitable to take on this role.

Complaints

Institutions offering doctoral programs need to have in place appropriate mechanisms for dealing with formal and informal expressions of student feedback about supervision, including official complaints mechanisms. For disputes that cannot be resolved there should be provision for appeal to a final Third Party who is neutral and external to the institution, and who understands academic process. If as a supervisor you find yourself in the unfortunate position of being the subject of a student complaint, it is important to handle it with professionalism as well as spiritual maturity and grace. Cooperate fully with the process, and listen to the complaint and what lies behind it. There can be a temptation for academics to 'close ranks', but if a student has a concern it should be heard properly and dealt with fairly. If mistakes have been made, then it is the Christian supervisor's responsibility to offer appropriate apologies, and seek forgiveness. Work to remedy problems that have been identified. If the complaint is found to be without foundation, that too should be handled with the appropriate spiritual maturity, and with a spirit of willingness to forgive. If you are to continue working with the student, the process should not be allowed to cloud a proper working relationship being continued.

Supervisor Responsibilities

The institution running a doctoral program should have in place written guidance on what the responsibilities of all research student supervisors.

Choice of Supervisor

The allocation of students to supervisors is an institutional decision, but it should be made in consultation with the student and you as the intended supervisor. The crucial factor has to be a close correspondence between the student's research field, and your area of research competence as a supervisor. Where this is not found, another supervisor should be chosen. Allocation should not be made on the grounds of giving the student to the supervisor who has the lowest supervisory load and therefore some spare capacity, nor should it be based on who is the most popular supervisor. In some cultures the most senior academic faculty in terms of age and experience select the best students for themselves, but while these factors should be respected, the best fit between the student's need and the supervisor's gifting remains paramount. In these situations, depending on the role you play, you might need to exercise patience or grace.

It is important to understand and respect the institution's process for supervisor allocation. It is in the student's best interest to identify the likely supervisor of an intended thesis / dissertation at the earliest opportunity. Sometimes students build a relationship with a likely supervisor during the application process, and can then be frustrated when a different supervisor is allocated on acceptance. Similarly a supervisor can spend significant time working with, and shaping the approach of a potential student, only to find that the student is allocated to another supervisor, which is disappointing. To avoid this, clarity and transparency of process and communication is very important.

Supervisory Teams / Dissertation Committees

Normally, a doctoral student on the thesis component of a doctoral program will have more than one supervisor. When this is the case they work together as part of a supervisory team, or on US-style programs the student interacts with a dissertation committee. To avoid confusion about what is expected of the different members of the supervisory team / dissertation committee, institutions need to ensure that the responsibilities of research supervisors, committee chairs, and second / third readers, are clearly communicated to supervisors and students through written guidance. These should be agreed by all the supervisors, and signed by them and the head of the program and the student.

The creation of supervisory teams / dissertation committees means the student has access to the best range of expertise, especially if the project has interdisciplinary elements. It also ensures continuity of support for a student if a member of the team is on research leave or unable to provide support for a period of time such as through illness. Supervisory teams sometimes include second supervisors / readers who are not in possession of a doctorate. Such individuals need to be experienced teachers at postgraduate level with detailed and subject-specific academic currency. Their role is to support the work of the main supervisor.

Normally the lead supervisor / chair of dissertation committee should be a member of academic faculty in the institution where the doctoral program is being delivered, but sometimes supervisory teams include members from other academic institutions. If you are the lead supervisor / chair of dissertation committee, it is important that you ensure a good flow of information between the other team members.

As a doctoral supervisor, I have served as the primary supervisor, and also on occasion as a second supervisor. In each case, different approaches are needed. Operating as part of a supervisory team can be an enriching and mutually beneficial dimension of academic work. It is a privilege to work closely with other colleagues, some of whom have been world leaders in their field, and from which much can be learned. But it is a relationship that requires mutual respect, trust, understanding, humility and sensitivity. There are cases where one member of the team 'takes over', and sidelines other members of the team. Sometimes decisions are made, and advice given, without the other members of the supervisory team being informed.

Some supervisors feel threatened, or undermined, by being part of a team, and the value of each team member needs to be regularly affirmed. With mutual respect and understanding this can be avoided. Clarity of communication, and a well-established process in which all have confidence, are essential. The first supervisor / chair of dissertation committee must ensure that clear and regular communication between members of the committee is maintained.

The overriding need is for students to have a positive and enriching experience of being supervised. Sadly, as student feedback from a variety of contexts shows, this is not always the case.

However, the expectation and behavior of doctoral students who are supervised by a team also needs to be managed. Some students will try and play one supervisor / reader off against another to get the advice they would like to hear, or less onerous standards. For this reason, members of supervisory teams should be copied into correspondence between the primary supervisor and the student, and comments on work should be similarly shared. Decisions on direction, key methods, and recommendations on progression issues should be genuine team decisions, reached by discussion and consensus.

Remember the Privilege of Supervision

This chapter has covered many matters of routine and process. Through the administrative demands that come with supervising research, never forget the privilege it is to supervise research students. Always remember to be excited that:

- Someone has chosen to undertake research in your area.
- Someone has chosen to undertake research work supervised by you – recognising that you are a leading authority in this field.

As you embark on this process, think through how you will, through all the demands of the process, supervise in such a way that students become as enthusiastic, engaged, willing to work hard, and keen to teach in your subject area as you are. How will you get your research students to love the subject as much as you do?

Case Study

It is well known by yourself and among your academic colleagues that a member of the faculty who is a supervisor is very bad at completing progression forms and reports. They lie incomplete on his desk for months at a time, despite repeated requests to complete them. He is otherwise a good teacher and amenable colleague. Review boards are delayed because he has not completed the paperwork. One important form was only completed because the postgraduate studies leader stood over him while he did it. It has become a matter for verbal complaints by students.

Questions

What do you think lies at the heart of this problem?

In order to enhance student experience, what can you and your colleagues do to help remedy this situation?

Further Reading

Eley, A., and R. Murray. *How to Be an Effective Supervisor*. Maidenhead: Open University Press, 2009.

Phillips, E. M., and D. S. Pugh. *How to Get a PhD: A Handbook for Students and Their Supervisors*. Maidenhead: Open University Press, 2010. (Kindle edition available also.)

Shaw, I. *Best Practice Guidelines for Doctoral Programs*. Carlisle: Langham Global Library, 2015.

Taylor, S., and N. Beasley. *A Handbook for Doctoral Supervisors*. New York: Routledge, 2005.

Wisker, Gina. *The Good Supervisor: Supervising Postgraduate and Undergraduate Research for Doctoral Theses and Dissertations*. New York: Palgrave MacMillan, 2005.

14

Common Problem Areas

Sometimes the supervisory relationship runs smoothly, and the experience is positive all round. However, problems can occur, and it is good to have thought through a series of appropriate responses before challenging events arise. The following are some of the most common issues that are encountered in dealing with doctoral students.

Problem Area 1: Plagiarism

> *Institutional regulations and program guidance need to set out clearly that all source material is to be acknowledged and fully referenced, and the form in which such references will be presented. Plagiarism reflects not only academic weaknesses, but also moral and spiritual failings. Warnings against plagiarism must be highlighted in institutional regulations and program guidance, together with details of the sanctions that will be imposed if plagiarism is detected in a doctoral thesis / dissertation.*[1]

Even at masters and doctoral level, plagiarism needs to be warned about, watched for, and guarded against. The doctoral thesis is to be an 'original contribution to knowledge', and where a student's work consists in part, or even in its entirety, of material from other sources that are not acknowledged, this is a serious matter. It betrays not only academic failings, but weaknesses in educational method and also spiritual formation. Plagiarism is academic theft, and something that evangelical students and supervisors need to take seriously.

1) What Does Plagiarism Entail?

Plagiarism is the use of materials from a source written by someone else, without acknowledging its origin. That source can include a book, article, Internet source, or

---

1. Shaw, *Best Practice*, Section 19.

another thesis. All sources used by students need to be fully acknowledged, even when not directly quoted, and their use supported by an appropriate reference.

When a student is quoting the actual words of a source, those words need to be enclosed in quotation marks, and fully referenced. The quotation marks should enclose the whole of the verbatim quote, otherwise the impression is given that the rest of the quote is the student's own work.

When students summarize, or paraphrase, the ideas from another source, even if it is not directly quoted, they need to be referenced clearly, to indicate their source. These are not the student's own thoughts, but a summary of those of someone else.

2) Forms of Plagiarism

Plagiarism can take a variety of forms:

i) **It can be unwitting.** This may be the result of the academic culture in which students have been trained, so they do not realize this is a serious issue. Students need to understand that referencing is a sign of good academic practice, not of bad dependence or academic weakness. They should celebrate the wide reading they have done, and demonstrate it in the synthesis, allusions, quotations and references they use. For this they will be commended. It is possible for even experienced academics who have taken notes on their reading, to find when they come to use their notes for an article or book sometime later, to be unsure exactly what was the words of their source, and what was their own personal reflection on that source. So diligence in making such distinctions in gathering sources is most important. Others may copy material from a source, especially an electronic one, and forget to include a reference to its origin. However, accurate note taking and identification of all sources through good referencing remains at the heart of good academic practice, and all writers should double check their work for these issues.

ii) **It can be deliberate.** Sadly, even in evangelical contexts, students can be tempted to deliberately try and mislead their supervisors, and their examiners, by trying to pass off parts of what they submit, or in extreme cases all of it, as if it is their own work, when it has come from others. Some plagiarism is a very carefully planned attempt at deception. It can involve obtaining papers online, or even asking external writers to write work for them. While this is less likely to be done at research doctoral level, where the supervisor has regular interaction with an evolving piece of work, it remains possible, and supervisors should watch for this. Doctoral programs without an oral examination involving at least one external assessor, in which the examiners have opportunity to satisfy themselves that the piece of work is the student's own, need to be especially vigilant.

Cut-and-paste style plagiarism is more common, taking a range of unattributed materials from e-resources, websites, or in the old-fashioned way from books and articles.

iii) **It varies in degrees and sanctions.** Occasional slips, and inadequate referencing, can be challenged without serious sanction. However, repeated and large-scale occurrences need to be treated with serious sanctions. These should be set out in institutional academic regulations.

3) *Plagiarism Has a Number of Causes*

Students cheat for all sorts of reasons. With such large amounts of material available online, it is a failure increasingly easy to commit, and supervisors need to be ever vigilant.

It can be a product of lack of time. A student under pressure may find large amounts of material in another source, and to save time simply repeat it. In using electronic resources this is easily done.

It can be a product of poor academic training. Some students come from academic backgrounds where the issue is not highlighted, and the supervisor needs to work to instil proper referencing skills.

It can reflect cultural issues. For students educated in a rote learning culture, where there is high respect for the teacher and an unwillingness to disagree, students can find it hard to understand what is wrong with plagiarism – surely, they think, it is honoring the scholar to copy their work. Again, this needs to be challenged and corrected.

It can be a product of academic weakness, or lack of confidence. A scholarly source covers an issue in a way that the student feels they cannot improve upon, so they simply repeat it word for word. Supervisors need to show students how to find their own academic voice.

At root, it is also a spiritual issue. It is academic fraud. It is taking what does not belong to you – someone else's ideas and research work – and using it without permission and for your own advancement. It is a form of theft, and breaks the eighth of the Ten Commandments. It demonstrates a failure to love your neighbor, and respect his (intellectual) property. On academic and spiritual formation grounds it needs to be challenged early and consistently, and the student made aware of the range of sanctions against it.

4) *Students Need Teaching on the Proper Way to Paraphrase, Summarize and Synthesize Material*

Studies suggest that careful instruction and guidance about the issue of plagiarism does reduce its incidence. Furthermore, those with the highest propensity to plagiarize are most likely to drop out of their course.[2]

Students need to know the difference between paraphrasing and summarizing, and copying a continuous section of text without quotation marks or reference. They need to learn how to mix paraphrase and direct quotation, and provide the appropriate references in the right places. But the difference between poor style and deliberate cheating can be hard to judge.

When a student paraphrases material from a source, but doesn't directly quote it, and then doesn't give a citation, this is still plagiarism. Students need to acknowledge every instance where they use work, ideas, research materials, statistics, that are not their own. Some students just substitute one or two words in a piece of text they are copying and think that by doing that they are making it their 'own' work, but this remains unacceptable.

5) *Proper Citation*

Many students enter doctoral programs with an inadequate understanding of the method of, and reason for, proper citation of sources. They need to see the importance of adequate references for a range of 'good practice' reasons:

- It shows the sources they have used – thus avoiding accusations of plagiarism.
- It helps the reader easily locate the source the writer has used if they wish to consult it.
- It shows that arguments advanced are based on an adequate basis of reading, and that the writer interacts with sources at the right level. Students need to show they are familiar with the language of academic discourse in their field, and references and bibliography serve to demonstrate that.
- It shows respect for the intellectual capital of others. As academic work is increasingly being commoditized into intellectual property, the student needs to show respect to their academic peers, and in return expect respect to be shown to their work.

6) *Bibliographies*

Bibliographies should contain all material that has been consulted and assessed in writing the piece, not just what is quoted. Insisting on this ensures that students show the

---

2. M. E. Earman Stetter, 'Teaching Students about Plagiarism Using a Web-Based Module,' *Journal of Further and Higher Education* 37, no. 5 (2013): 675–693.

materials they have worked with, and helps the reader trace deliberate or unwitting use of unattributed material, and detect deliberate omissions.

7) Style Guides

While there is a need to give initial guidance, a lot of supervisory time can needlessly be spent correcting student's references. It is better to get the student to follow the style guide exactly, and point out where they have failed to do so. Supervisors should at an early stage require students to obtain a good style guide, such as the *Chicago Manual of Style*, which gives detailed guidance on citation, referencing, and bibliographical entries for a huge range of research material.

8) Detecting Plagiarism

i)   Plagiarism Detection Software

Technology is slowly catching up with the opportunities for plagiarism. Programs such as *Turnitin* require the student to submit work electronically, and when it is run through the program it rates the originality of what is written against the store of other academic work in its database. This helps students identify places where their work is overdependent on other sources.

What is measured:

- the total percentage of material copied / number of words copied verbatim divided by the total number of words in the essay.
- the number of separate word strings copied verbatim.
- the longest continuous portion of copied text.

This system requires all submissions of material to be made electronically. This can be quite onerous with doctoral work at its initial stages, but when fuller drafts are submitted it can be of value to highlight problem areas. If there is a major problem of overdependency on the work of others, it is better for it to be detected early, rather than at final submission stage, when it is too late to challenge, and only serious sanction remains.

ii) Limitations

However, even these measures may need to be supplemented with some forms of qualitative assessment. Use of plagiarism detection software does not eliminate all plagiarism. Internet technology does push towards a cut-and-paste approach to writing, and students can get round the plagiarism software issue by paraphrasing and rearranging material to avoid detection. So training and awareness remain vital.[3]

---

3. J. Warn, 'Plagiarism Software: No Magic Bullet!' *Higher Education Research and Development* 25, no. 2 (2006): 195–208.

Also, if a student quotes material in other languages, including accessing other masters and doctoral theses that are not entered in the software database, this can mean plagiarized sources can go undetected. Other dissertations and research work will need to be uploaded into software to extend the range of material for comparisons, and that does not always happen.

In some academic contexts, there is an encouragement for students to submit their work in a local or regional language. If examiners with high degrees of competence in those languages can be found, there can be merit in this. However, most plagiarism detection software only works with the major languages of academic discourse.

iii) Spotting Plagiarism

Even with the electronic helps available, supervisors need to remain vigilant, and watch for warning signs, as well as becoming familiar with the student's natural writing style. As a student interacts with a supervisor, you should look to see their skills and approach evolving.

Look for:

- Sudden changes in style. If you are familiar with the student's 'natural style', and a very different style suddenly appears in a section, this should be investigated.
- Appearance of ideas and findings that seem out of the range you would expect the student to have achieved at that point.
- Material that is well written, but not directly relevant to the point being discussed.
- Long and unexplained absences on the part of the student followed by the sudden appearance of well-developed work.

9) Sanctions for Plagiarism

Institutions should provide clear statements on what constitutes plagiarism, the sanctions that will be applied when it is detected, proper training courses to help students avoid the failing, and where possible the use of electronic resources to identify cases where it has happened.

The sanctions should fit the nature of the offense. These can range from the request to rewrite certain sections, to formal warnings, and the possibility of outright failure. If minor problems are detected these should be quickly highlighted and corrected. If this persists as thesis drafts are being submitted, the matter should be reported to the leader of the postgraduate studies / research program, and where necessary to the relevant academic board.

For doctoral programs, which include coursework, the sanction for infringements of plagiarism at each stage needs to be highlighted, and consistently applied.

If major plagiarism is detected, such that a large part of the thesis is not the student's own work, it is within the capacity of the examiners to fail the thesis outright.

Key Issues

Recent studies[4] highlight the importance of:

i)   Open discussion with groups of research students about the issue, and helping students to identify the potential problem areas.

ii) Classes and instruction on how to paraphrase, and getting students to undertake practical tests to show how they have applied this material.

iii) Proper referencing and citation guidance.

iv) Clear direction on use of web-based and electronic materials.

v)   Discussion of the moral issues of acknowledging other sources – how plagiarism is intellectual theft but also a spiritual failing.

Reflective Questions

How have you felt when you detected plagiarism in a student's work?

Which ways have you used to identify plagiarism? Which works best?

What can you do to ensure doctoral students do not make this mistake?

How do you address cultural, educational, and spiritual issues that might lie behind this?

Problem Area 2: How Much Should a Supervisor Correct Spelling and Grammatical Errors?

This is a question repeatedly asked in the seminars I run for training doctoral supervisors. The answers vary significantly between supervisors and cultures. Poor spelling and grammar even in early submissions of work can make them difficult to read and the argument hard to follow. The supervisor's attention is constantly distracted by the way the work is presented.

In assessing the extent to which such support is offered it is important to bear in mind that,

---

4. E.g. F. Duggan, 'Plagiarism: Prevention, Practice and Policy,' *Assessment & Evaluation in Higher Education* 31, no. 2 (2006): 151–154; R. Sharma, 'A Step-by-Step Guide to Students: How to Avoid Plagiarism,' *Journal of Education Research* 4, no. 2 (2010): 143–153; A. L. Walker, 'Preventing Unintentional Plagiarism: A Method for Strengthening Paraphrasing Skills,' *Journal of Instructional Psychology* 35, no. 4 (2007): 387–395.

i)   In the end, the thesis is, and must be, the student's work.

ii)   The supervisor's principal task is to assess content, structure, and academic standards, not be a professional spelling and grammar checker!

iii) Most students need help with writing – and because of this institutions should run writing skills courses to assist postgraduate writers.

iv)   Most supervisors will on the first submission of a piece of work offer basic corrections, but if extensive corrections are needed in subsequent pieces of work and the problems are repeated, it is usual to refer the work back to the student to be corrected before it is fully reviewed.

v)   It is useful for students to find a critical friend who can read over their initial drafts, as long as they only comment on spelling, punctuation, grammar, clarity, and not content.

vi)   It is a good support to doctoral students to spend some time working with them on their regular progress reports which the institution requires. Time spent advising on presentation issues at this juncture can be a good investment.

Problem Area 3: What Is Original Work?

Sometimes original work is not welcomed:

> The 'telephone' has too many shortcomings to be seriously considered as a means of communication. The device has inherently no value to us. (Western Union Memo, 1876)

> But who is going to want to hear the actors talking in movies? (HM Warner, Warner Brothers, 1927)

The issue of originality can be a significant preoccupation for doctoral students. In the ICETE *Beirut Benchmarks*, doctoral level work is described as 'a creative and original contribution that extends the frontiers of knowledge.'[5]

Sometimes it is unclear what 'original' means – and in some fields it is hard to be original, where all key topics have been researched already. The *Beirut Benchmarks* amplify the reference to 'creative and original', by explaining further – 'or develops fresh insights in the articulation and contextual relevance of the Christian tradition, some of which merit national or international refereed publication.'

---

5. 'ICETE Beirut Benchmarks,' in *Best Practice*, ed. I. Shaw, Section 1, Benchmark 4.

Originality can be quite a broad concept, and can be demonstrated in a variety of ways. It can be simply 'writing about something that nobody has written about before', but it may be a new synthesis, or a new interpretation of the ideas of others. It can be applying an approach in a context where it has never been attempted before, or using a previously used technique in a new academic field. The student might be testing existing knowledge in an original way, or developing a research idea from someone else, and taking it further and in new directions. It can involve bringing new evidence to bear on an old issue. Interdisciplinary approaches can open up new fields and new insights.

Reflective Questions

What were the original dimensions of your thesis?

What aspects of originality do you see in the work of your current research students?

If a student's work is largely derivative, how can you increase the level of originality in their work?

Problem Area 4: Supporting Students Working in Another Language to Their Own

This is another area that has regularly been raised and discussed in doctoral training seminars, and causes significant challenges for supervisors. When a student struggles with oral or written communication in the language in which the program is being delivered, and in which the thesis will be written, it adds significant workload and stress to the supervisor.

This means that there needs to be close agreement on policy and practice between those admitting students onto the doctoral program, and those delivering it. Sometimes supervisors feel they are left to 'pick up the pieces' when the institution has admitted students who lack the required language skills.

Doctoral programs need to operate on the principle that all students should be treated the same, even if the program is not offered in the student's first language. If a student has chosen to study in an English, or German, or French, or Chinese, etc., medium program they should not expect special allowances or lower academic standards to apply if that is not their first language.

Students need the required oral and written skills in the language of the program in order to progress through it and successfully undergo examination. Their examiners must be able to understand what they are writing or saying if there is an oral component.

Some useful principles:

i)   There should be benchmarks for acceptable language levels for course entry, and these need to be consistently applied. Usually these are set according to scores attained in internationally recognized language tests.

ii) The supervisor should show sympathy and understanding for those working and writing in a language not their own, but should not place excessive burdens on themselves to help the student deal with language deficit, and should not compromise on academic standards. Where significant support is needed, the student should be referred by them on to appropriate professional language skills courses.

iii) Once a student is accepted and has passed the entry criteria, it is the responsibility of the institution to give them the help they need. It is therefore vital that the required standard is appropriately rigorous. Supervisors should also play a significant role in the admission of students they will supervise, ensuring that from the outset the student has the language skills to succeed.

iv) Supervisors should work out what the culturally accepted communication forms are, and adapt their style to take account of them.

v)   Help students from other language backgrounds and educational cultures to see the learning culture expected at doctoral level means the supervisor can only give limited support.

vi) When supervising students from another language background, encourage them to ask questions of you. Sometimes you need to ask them to repeat back your instructions to ensure they have understood what is asked of them. If the student is silent, or asks limited questions, this does not imply full understanding, and sometimes the exact opposite.

vii) Encourage students from other language backgrounds to debate and dialogue with other students in the language of the program, and present work orally whenever they can. Try and give feedback on these occasions – stressing the importance of clarity and audibility – better 500 words that are audible than 1,000 words which are inaudible or incoherent. Students need to know how many words they can present from a script in the time allotted, and practice their delivery style.

Problem Area 5: Finance

As we saw in chapter 6, doing a doctorate is a very expensive business. One of the biggest causes of non-completion is lack of finance to finish the project. Sometimes a promised sponsor drops out, or the time commitment for funding runs out before the project is finished. Many students have unrealistic expectations of the cost of doctoral study, and never had enough funds to start in the first place, which makes the planning and review chapter in this book very important.

There is also the difficulty of gauging how long it will take to complete the research and writing of a thesis, especially in subjects where extensive field or archive research is required. Lack of funds causes significant stress, and can lead to students taking on extra paid work to make up any shortfall, which gives them even less time for study.

Supervisors react to these issues in different ways. I have known supervisors who have gone to great lengths to secure further funding for students, and even cases of them paying electricity bills from their own funds to help students through. This is of course a matter of personal choice, and is not a required part of being a supervisor!

Reflective Questions

What institutional provisions are in place to help students in financial need?

How does dealing with a student facing financial issues change the type of supervision offered?

What preventative action can you and your study institution put in place to avoid students encountering serious financial problems?

Problem Area 6: Family and Health Issues

In a doctoral program lasting four years or more, a lot of 'life events' will happen, and the supervisor needs to be prepared for these eventualities.

Doctoral students and their families tend to be young, so there may be additional members of the family born during doctoral study. At the least this will mean sleepless nights, and extra finance for food, clothing and schooling, but the birth of a child can be a major stress event, which can disrupt doctoral studies considerably. For women in particular there will be a need to take a suspension of studies for a period late in pregnancy, and after the birth of a child. The impact on studies can be quite considerable. Some women adapt to these extra challenges very smoothly, but in other cases they can lead to lengthy study breaks, or even the abandonment of the doctoral program.

As part of pastoral care it can be helpful to talk through these issues honestly at the start of a student's program, and the question of the best time to plan family additions sensitively raised.

Childcare can be a considerable challenge for students studying away from home, and in other cultures. Without the normal support structures of family, making suitable arrangements to care for children who are out of school, or taking them to school, can be very difficult. This is increased if a student's spouse is working. Students need to be helped to get a proper life balance. Because they are not in paid employment does not mean they are free to take on full-time child care as well as doctoral studies – indeed, the doctorate should be seen as effectively a full-time job. Other students are so busy studying, they hardly have time for their families, who begin to feel resentful of their comparative neglect. It is helpful for the supervisor to talk these issues through from time to time.

Most students will have elderly relatives. In some cultures the duty to personally care for them is very strong. There are the challenges of relatives who fall seriously ill, and there may be bereavements to face. The supervisor needs to be prepared that life events go on throughout the doctoral studies, and appropriate adjustments made and advice given.

Undertaking a doctoral program can be extremely stressful, and sometimes students need to be advised to seek medical help for this. Stress adds to physical pressures on the body. Many students will experience a period of illness during their studies. Supervisory regimes need to be flexible enough to take account of periodic breaks for illness, and have appropriate processes in place when this happens.

Reflective Questions

What institutional provisions are in place to support students facing the 'life issues' described above?

Are you familiar with the processes required for suspension of studies due to ill-health, childbirth, bereavements, etc?

How does facing these 'life issues' change the type of supervision to be offered?

Case Study

Samuel has been very difficult to pin down for regular supervision meetings for his masters dissertation. When you ask him what he is doing he speaks generally about his research, but does not talk about it in any detail. He has produced a short introduction, which was not a strong piece of work, and an outline of another chapter. The submission deadline is fast approaching, and the rest of the chapters have not appeared. When you do manage to meet with him Samuel mutters something about how he will soon have something ready, and then he is not in touch with you for several weeks. His friends do not know where he is, just that he is out of town. On the deadline day he appears with a full dissertation, which appears well presented, but the title has changed somewhat from what you discussed and the introduction has been altered. Three new chapters have been produced which are much better than the original introduction, but the style in which they are written seems different from the one Samuel has used in the introduction. The line of argument does not fit together through the dissertation. When you ask him where he has been, he says he found some good ideas in the library of a seminary some distance away, and once he had these, the thesis came together quickly.

When you think about this situation, something does not seem right.

Questions

Analyze the evidence before you in this case.

What should you as supervisor do in this situation?

What should your institution do in a case like this?

What should you say to Samuel?

Further Reading

Duggan, F. 'Plagiarism: Prevention, Practice and Policy.' *Assessment & Evaluation in Higher Education* 31, no. 2 (2006): 151–154.

Embleton, K., and D. S. Helfer. 'The Plague of Plagiarism and Academic Dishonesty.' *Searcher* 15, no.6 (2007): 23–26.

Lancaster, T., and F. Culwin. 'Preserving Academic Integrity – Fighting Against Non-Originality Agencies.' *British Journal of Educational Technology* 38, no. 1 (2007): 153–157.

Nitterhouse, D. 'Plagiarism – Not Just an 'Academic' Problem.' *Teaching Business Ethics* 7, no. 3 (2003): 215–227.

Sharma, R. 'A Step-by-Step Guide to Students: How to Avoid Plagiarism.' *Journal of Education Research* 4, no. 2 (2010): 143–153.

Walker, A. L. 'Preventing Unintentional Plagiarism: A Method for Strengthening Paraphrasing Skills.' *Journal of Instructional Psychology* 35, no. 4 (2007): 387–395.

Warn, J. 'Plagiarism Software: No Magic Bullet!' *Higher Education Research and Development* 25, no. 2 (2006): 195–208.

15

Supporting and Developing Doctoral Students Holistically

Evangelicals have a strong and abiding commitment to the person and work of Christ, and give particular emphasis to key teachings about him, and about God's revelation in the Bible. The hope of an evangelical research supervisor is that through undertaking doctoral studies, the commitment of students to these beliefs is strengthened, deepened, and enriched.

However, John Stott used to urge evangelical students undertaking doctoral studies of the need for growth in 'academic excellence and personal godliness at the same time'. He warned of the danger of returning home to church or seminary after three or four years 'an academic success but a spiritual failure, a "doctor" (qualified to teach) but no longer a "disciple", possessed by no new vision, power, or holiness'. He was fond of quoting Bishop Handley Moule's aphorism, 'Beware of an untheological devotion and of an undevotional theology'. Stott also pointed students to T. F. Torrance's understanding of theological study as a form of 'intense intellectual communion with God, in which our minds are taken captive by his love and we come to know God more and more through himself'. He urged evangelical doctoral students to become not only competent teachers of theology, but also people who will 'truly know and worship the God they talk about'.[1]

Sadly, some of those who have the opportunity to research most closely into Scripture, or explore key theological issues, have found their deeply held faith challenged by what they read. Some have abandoned the evangelical theological convictions they once cherished, and embraced liberal theology, or have failed to sustain patterns of lifestyle and morality that are recognizably evangelical.

---

1. 'An Admonition from John Stott,' *Fellowship of Langham Scholars Newsletter,* no. 2, April 1996. See also the author's personal notes of Langham Scholars Orientation course, Oxford Centre for Mission Studies, September 1993, which the author attended as a grantee of the Whitefield Institute.

This places significant emphasis on the evangelical supervisor of doctoral students to be a wise teacher, counsellor, and friend, so that engagement with the challenges of academic theology does not result in a deconstruction of a PhD student's personal faith.

Academic Freedom and Personal Faith Commitment

The issue of the connection between the academic freedom to research and explore key areas without artifical constraint and limitation, which lies at the heart of the research exercise at doctoral level, can create challenges to those personally committed to a position of confessional orthodoxy, or working in a context where confessional orthodoxy is carefully defined. It is important that each institution has a clearly defined statement on academic freedom, and that supervisors understand and work within that.

Academic 'freedom' is the openness to subject all ideas to honest enquiry. The ability to conduct genuine intellectual inquiry, and freedom of expression in communicating the fruits of that, is essential in an institution of higher education. Creating a context of 'academic freedom' means producing an environment in which all ideas, even those most cherished within a theological tradition, are open to discussion. In an institution offering doctoral studies, and promoting a research culture, the widest possible range of scholarship needs to be both encouraged and supported. Research students and faculty who engage in research need to be free to do this according to their own conscience and convictions. The freedom to enquire, and exercise individual critical judgment according to the dictates of conscience before God, which was such an important value in the Reformation, remains important to personal spiritual growth and responsibility.

If this exercise of individual judgment produces opinions that are new, or at variance with traditional perspectives, they should not be 'censored' or penalized, but instead thoroughly tested to see if they are put forward with intellectual rigor and sound argument, with proper appeal to evidence, and whether they are based on correct interpretation of Scripture. If they fail such tests, they should be challenged with fairness and grace as part of a serious commitment to understand the mind of God on a matter more clearly. In popular terms, theological kites can be flown to see how far they will go, but students should do this with an openness to being shown if there is a fault in the argument or the appeal to evidence, or if Scripture has not been handled properly. Indeed, there should be a welcome to being shown where the weaknesses lie.

Alongside this, there should be a recognition that the academic investigation should not be undertaken in isolation. For both student and supervisor, research activity must be exercised responsibly alongside the duties of professional and pastoral care for other students, academic competence in teaching and research, and willingness to subject one's own work to the scrutiny of others. If the student is undertaking research in an institution whose purpose is the training of individuals for the Christian ministry, then the need to uphold its ethos and values should not be ignored. This means that in colleges with confessional foundations, academic freedom needs to operate alongside confessional responsibility. Academic freedom can create tensions with personal commitment – no scholar is absolutely neutral. Yet, scholars with confessional or apologetic motivations can still undertake academic research and construct a thesis using proper academic argumentation, just as lawyers, who may have their own views on a matter, constantly investigate cases using proper judicial process to prove a case. Our theological commitments should be open to honest examination and evaluation against the standard of Scripture itself. Academic research should be allowed to run its course. However, those intent on undertaking research that is directly at variance with the purpose and theological commitments of the institution in which it is undertaken might be more comfortable undertaking that in another context. These sorts of issues should be identified by the admissions team and prospective supervisor when a prospective student applies and is interviewed or engages in dialogue before entry, to ensure a good fit of backgrounds and expectations. In some cases a supervisor might advise a prospective student to seek a context where a certain topic or approach would work more naturally.[2]

The Proper Context for Theological Studies – The Wider Church

John Stott did not do a research doctorate, but the high academic merit of his detailed biblical and theological scholarship earned him the Lambeth Palace Doctor of Divinity degree. He combined scholarly ability with a warm and earnest evangelical commitment to Christ, the Bible, and deep integrity of personal faith. He knew the challenges to faith of academic study of theology, and spoke of the 'openness and commitment' tension at some length.

> We need to encourage Christian scholars to go to the frontiers and engage in the debate, while at the same time retaining their active participation in the community of believers. I know this is a delicate issue, and it is not easy to define the right relations between free enquiry and settled faith. Yet I have often been disturbed by the loneliness of some Christian scholars. Whether it is they who have drifted away from the fellowship, or the fellowship which has allowed them to drift, in either case their isolation is an unhealthy and dangerous condition. As part of their own integrity Christian scholars need both to preserve the tension between openness and commitment, and to accept some measure of accountability to one another and responsibility for one another in the body of Christ. In such a caring fellowship I think

---

2. This summary is based on the statement of Moore College, an Anglican training college in Sydney, Australia.

we might witness fewer casualties on the one hand and more theological creativity on the other.[3]

Evangelical supervisors and their doctoral researchers must find ways of living within this tension of being at the 'frontiers' of academic debate, and 'active participation in the community of faith.' Doctoral students need the freedom to discuss these issues, and they need to have good examples to follow. John Stott's words highlight the danger of the scholar drifting away from the fellowship of the church. Sadly there are times when this has happened to evangelical research students. I am convinced that Stott is right when he argued that rootedness in the church fellowship, will result in more theological creativity and fewer casualties. This issue needs to be seriously addressed by supervisors. The 'lone ranger' scholar without the mutual support and accountability a local church provides, is in a dangerous situation.

I was struck recently by the resolute response of a doctoral student studying in a theological department in a South African university which was predominantly liberal, when I asked him about this issue:

> I have godly people in my home country who have sacrificially given finances
> and time to invest in me, and I owe it to them to come back sound in the faith
> without having given in to this liberalism.

What is even more distressing is to see doctoral supervisors, who are models for such students, but who have drifted from involvement with a local church, and may even have ceased attendance at it. They speak openly about how they are totally disillusioned with the church. This is more common than might be imagined.

While this is a serious anomaly that some of those preparing others for leadership in the church have themselves opted out of local church life, I also rejoice that I have seen opposite to be true as well. I know of renowned academics at the most prestigious theological institutions faithfully serving as elders and deacons, taking their turn on the preaching rota, leading home Bible study groups, and enthusiastically engaged in sharing the gospel with children and young people.

It can be difficult for academically gifted theologians to listen to the preaching of ministers who know far less than they do, and whose sermons are not well-developed theologically, or who do not handle the biblical text as thoroughly as they might wish. It can be a challenge to relate to lay believers whose understanding of the faith is very simple, if not simplistic. When his theological students complained about ordinary church life, Martin Luther observed:

---

3. J. Stott, *I Believe in Preaching* (London, Hodder and Stoughton, 1982), 87.

> People cannot have their ministers exactly as they wish . . . they should thank God that they have the pure word and not demand St Augustines and St Ambroses to preach it to them. If a pastor pleases the Lord Jesus and is faithful to him, – there is none so great and mighty that he ought to be pleased with him, too.[4]

Maybe the local church is not the place the doctoral supervisor will find the deep teaching we all long for, yet the Scripture remains clear on this matter, and is as applicable to a Christian seminary professor as to a Christian plumber or window cleaner – 'Let us not give up meeting together, as some are in the habit of doing, but let us encourage one another – and all the more as you see the Day approaching.'[5] As the writer of *Hebrews* highlights, there is far more to belonging to the local church than receiving deep and challenging teaching, much though this is to be desired. The local church brings the mutual prayer support, love, encouragement, and kindness of fellow believers, which is rich indeed. But there are also opportunities for service and 'encouragement' towards others. Local church pastors may be nervous about having theological professors in their congregations, and need encouraging. The sick need visiting, the visitor needs hospitality. The doctoral supervisor or research student should not be above leading a house group, teaching a Sunday school class, serving on the coffee rota, or joining the church cleaning day. Our model is Christ who debated with the learned scribes in the temple courts, yet also washed the feet of his disciples.

Reflective Questions

How would you assess your engagement with a local church?

What opportunities have you to serve in that local community?

Where did you find was the major problem area as research student in relating to your local church community?

How has being rooted in a local church helped you in your scholarly and Christian life?

What would you most like to change?

---

4. Luther, quoted in Warfield, *Theological Studies*, 190.

5. Hebrews 10:25.

Dealing with Theological Problem Areas

It is important for doctoral supervisors to be open about the problem issues in their discipline with students. There is sometimes a strange silence on the part of supervisors that leaves students wondering if problem areas should be talked about at all, and whether there is permission to do so. This reticence leaves doctoral students ill-equipped to handle these issues in the future, and lacking the appropriate language of discourse with which to address them.

Be Clear on Scripture

Many evangelical students studying Scripture at doctoral level do not have a clear doctrine of Scripture. Although working closely on the text, they keep this quite separate from their doctrinal views. This seems strange.

Reflective Questions

What is your own doctrine of Scripture?

How is that shaped by your institutional context – and what tensions does that context create?

How might you explain this to a doctoral student exploring their own views on Scripture?

Tackling the Tough Issues

John Stott reflected openly on the challenges he faced when studying theology in the predominantly theologically liberal atmosphere of Cambridge University in the 1940s. Stott often found himself the only evangelical in the whole class while lecturers outlined their liberal approaches with confidence and assurance. To Stott this brought severe 'pain in the mind' as he sought to find answers to these arguments, and maintain with intellectual rigor his evangelical position and demonstrate to his own satisfaction that it was true. If anyone read theology in such a context, and survived with their core evangelical convictions in tact, it was considered a 'miracle' – and Stott was one such. What maintained him was his relentless certainty that in order to challenge those who would undermine the evangelical understanding of the gospel he needed to answer them at their own level of scholarship. Whenever he came across an issue that perplexed him or challenged his faith, he worked and prayed relentlessly on the matter until he found what he believed was a satisfactory solution. He was also helped by having a close friend with whom he shared and discussed issues – Douglas Johnson, who became a key leader in InterVarsity Fellowship, later UCCF.[6]

Don't Let Small Issues Overturn Big Convictions

High-level theological study will raise profound challenges at some point. How the research student reacts at those points is crucial. Speaking at the Langham Scholar Consultation at Cambridge University in 2011 one well-known biblical scholar spoke of the challenges he faced when researching and writing in his own discipline:

> There are times when I encounter an issue in the study of Scripture that challenges my evangelical convictions. At that moment I have a choice. Will I pursue that issue so that it potentially undermines my deeply held convictions, or do I consciously choose to see that my faith and doctrinal position is bigger than this issue, and leave the matter, albeit unresolved, until I am able to understand it further? Persistent preoccupation with that small issue may cause me to magnify it beyond its significance, and ultimately do me spiritual harm. Whereas, if I have the courage to leave the issue on one side for now, often, and in time, with mature thought and study I find that the Lord has indeed fresh light to bring forth, and in the future a satisfactory solution becomes clear to me.

Know the Consequences of Crossing Boundaries

Another image I have sometimes heard used to understand the balance between academic freedom and personal confessional convictions, is that of the swimming pool. Christian convictions and historic confessional statements about doctrine and lifestyle create secure boundary lines within which to swim. Inside them there is freedom to move in many directions, and explore many options. However, when the boundary of the pool is touched, whether on a doctrinal or even a moral or lifestyle matter, the scholar now has a choice. This is whether to turn back and use their freedom to move in another direction, or whether to use their freedom to climb out. Most chose to swim in another direction and subsequently return to the point that had previously troubled them, and with fresh thoughts find it is not an issue any more – their understanding has changed and they can see it in a different or more mature way. Sometimes people choose to climb out. Many who do so walk away from the core values of the faith. One of the pioneers of modern New Testament critical studies, David F. Strauss, made such a choice and lost his personal faith completely and died refusing a Christian burial. The ranks of liberal scholars are regularly supplemented by evangelicals who have given up their core beliefs.

---

6. T. D. Smith, *John Stott, The Making of a Leader* (Downers Grove: InterVarsity Press, 1999), 180–203.

Occasionally, at 'pool-edge', boundary moments, fresh perspectives may come that can lead to new understandings of the pool, such as when Martin Luther broke free of the confessional limitations of medieval Catholicism, precipitating the Reformation.

Supporting Students in the Critical Moments

One of the tasks the evangelical supervisor should be willing to embrace, is supporting scholars at these critical moments. Many evangelicals have made potentially significant or devastating choices without a dialogue partner to assist them. In the spirit of commitment to open academic enquiry, discussion of complex and faith-challenging issues should not be forbidden as in some church traditions, but supported with wisdom and discernment. The scholar needs to be enabled to think through the implications of any 'pool-edge' choices they might make, and gaining an external perspective on what they may be finding deeply troubling can be vital. Is this a Luther-moment, or a D. F. Strauss-moment? This involves supporting not only the intellectual journey, but also exploring how issues will impact personal faith, relationships with a local church community, even family and friendship. And through this process, the evangelical supervisor will of course pray that the student's faith is not weakened, but strengthened by the process.

Reflective Questions

What space do you create in supervisory sessions for discussing the problem areas in the discipline?

How comfortable are you about sharing with students the problems posed to your faith by these problem areas?

If you feel hesitancy about this, why is that so?

What do you need to change in this area?

When It Does or Does Not Work Out

In the commitment by the evangelical supervisor, and doctoral researcher, to live in the tension between 'openness and commitment,' there is of course danger. It is possible that, despite your support and prayer, a student may make choices that lead them to give up core evangelical convictions. But, refusal to permit raising difficult issues and frank discussion of them is also dangerous – potentially leading to an obscurantist faith, or a faith with a profound dichotomy between the mind and matters of faith. Students can be overwhelmed by the deeply troubling anxiety caused by big questions left unaddressed and unresolved that can in themselves undermine faith. In this the supervisor is a key point of reference, and must be prepared and equipped with responses, which means you need to think through potential issues yourself. It is not good practice to train medical doctors by only letting them see patients who are healthy and untroubled – they learn from the difficult cases. So too with the theologian. By being stretched and tested in the challenging areas there should come a deeper level of understanding and faith commitment.

This makes offering supervision to doctoral students one of the greatest privileges, and challenges in academic work. The close interaction needed with the student, and the skills the student learns, in some ways makes it the closest in pedagogical approach to the discipleship model Jesus employed. That is indeed a high example to follow, and can produce some of the most satisfactory and lasting results.

Reflective Questions

List the books and articles you would recommend to a student struggling with how to reconcile their evangelical convictions with specific biblical or theological issues.

Which person (other than yourself) would you recommend to a student as a mentor and dialogue partner when they face issues of challenge in these areas?

If your seminary has a chaplain, what role might they play in addressing the issues discussed in this chapter?

How can supervisors help each other in responding to student faith concerns?

Measuring and Assessing the Holistic Development of Doctoral Students

The evangelical supervisor will measure the 'success' of doctoral students in more than merely academic terms.

Reflective Questions

What is your greatest hope for your doctoral students?

How will you measure your success, or otherwise, apart from examination failure or success?

Assessing Key Skills, Achievement, and Progress

A core vision for the doctoral supervisor in an evangelical institution is to produce doctoral students who are motivated and empowered by a deeper appreciation of the evangelical Christian tradition; and have greater understanding and application of the thinking and practices of godly discipleship; a more extensive knowledge base; enhanced research and teaching skills; and greater capacity for original thought. If our doctoral students become teachers, we want them to have the ability to communicate effectively what they have discovered in classroom and professional settings, and work at the forefront of Christian thinking. When they have completed a doctorate, we want them to be able to continue to serve Christ faithfully and grow professionally.

Each student is different, with a unique set of strengths and interests.

Appendix 3 is a checklist of key skills and character competencies that can be used as a 'learning log', and discussed and marked up every twelve months to track progress as the student reaches each stage.[7] Students entering a course should be clear that this range of areas will be used to assess their overall progress.

Case Study

Dawn is a very able student who thinks deeply. Her doctoral thesis integrates areas of New Testament study and philosophy. As she delves further into the philosophical side of her study, which she greatly enjoys, she concentrates increasingly on philosophical approaches and begins to raise major questions about her approach to Scripture. She then shares with you that she has stopped reading her Bible devotionally because she does not feel the need to do so, and her attendance at church is becoming more irregular. This is causing tension with her husband who wishes to maintain regular family devotions. You begin to feel that although doing well academically, she is not progressing in her personal faith, and your concerns are growing.

Questions

What key issues does this raise?

What can you do to help her as a supervisor?

What should the institution do in a case like this?

---

7. A very good example of such a checklist being implemented is the McMaster Divinity School, *PhD Mastery Checklist*, which was kindly shared with the author by their faculty.

16

Preparing Doctoral Candidates for Examination

The culmination of the supervision process comes when the doctoral candidate's work is presented to a wider panel of experts for examination. This can be an exciting, but also stressful time, for both student and supervisor. The supervisor needs to remember that it is the candidate's work which is being examined, not the supervisor's. Yet, there is also a sense that for the candidate to do well, the supervisor needs to have done a good job. If the student fails, the supervisor will find herself / himself asking significant questions about whether the right sort of supervision was offered. The fact that most forms of doctoral examination allow for revision and rewriting after the examination process does allow for some problems to be rectified, but you do want it to go well.

The Right Time to Submit the Thesis

As part of regular supervision, it is important to work out the time when the thesis is likely to be ready. As the doctoral program draws to an end the student will begin to ask 'do you think the thesis is ready for submission?' The last months and weeks of supervising a research student can be very intensive for the supervisor.

The supervisor should read carefully the final draft, and make suggestions for further revision before it is submitted. This is a time for the student to polish, and revise, and rewrite. The student should not be thinking 'perhaps the examiners won't notice' if there are deficiencies or discrepancies. They will notice – that is their task!

In answer to the student's question about the best time for submission of a thesis, the proper answer is 'when it is ready'. However, the reality can be more complicated. The submission can be driven by the timeline of the program – there will be a deadline by which the thesis must be submitted. The student may have a job to return to, or a visa running out, which push the deadline forward. The funds a student has are probably running out, demanding submission be not delayed. The supervisor should regularly discuss all these issues with the student, so any deadlines and their practical circumstances are kept clearly in view.

If you do not have much experience of supervising doctoral students, it is good practice to consult with the other members of the supervisory team, or with a senior colleague who is an experienced supervisor, to get their feedback on whether the thesis is ready for submission. The annual reviews should have looked very carefully at the basic concepts, methodology, and intent of the study to be sure that the project is headed in the right direction, and major issues or problems should have been identified at that stage. However, some final evaluation before submission is important. Some institutions have a pre-viva, or 'confirmation of status' review at this point at which other members of the academic community are able to review a full draft of the thesis and identify any key issues for revision.

The academic process varies in different institutions, but usually the supervisor is required to give some form of approval for submission, which is confirmed by the person or committee that oversees the research program. When the supervisor gives assent to a proposal to submit a thesis, they should be clear that,

- A substantial and original piece of research work has been produced.
- The student has followed all the presentation and formatting conventions required.
- A defendable thesis is now ready for the examiners.
- The student is, in terms of their personal and academic development, prepared for that defense.

The Oral Defense When There Is a Thesis / Dissertation Committee

In many ways, the process of working toward the final dissertation defense in US-type programs is very similar to preparing for the proposal defense. The supervisor / dissertation committee chair will have used feedback from the proposal defense to guide the student through the development of the dissertation document, providing feedback on initial drafts of chapters or sections of chapters, and determining when it seems appropriate to share the more fully developed drafts with the committee members for their review. When the feedback of all committee members has been received and addressed in the development of a defense document, the time eventually comes when the student and chair agree that the dissertation is ready for a final defense. This defense should not move forward if any of the committee members feel that significant additional work is needed for any of the section drafts that they have reviewed.

Being Absolutely Sure

Once the thesis is submitted, there is no way back, so the student and supervisor / dissertation committee should as far as possible be confident that the thesis is ready. It is not good practice for a student to be humiliated by the experience of presenting a thesis that is hopelessly bad, or examiners being required to spend their time examining a thesis that has no chance of passing.

In some systems, it is possible for a student to submit a thesis against the advice of her or his supervisor(s). This is a scenario to be avoided, but in some exceptional cases, where relationships have broken down with supervisors (see ch. 3), a student can claim the right to have their thesis defended. In those cases, the examination should be conducted as fairly and rigorously as in every other situation. If it is possible, the examiners should not be informed before or during the examination that the thesis was submitted without the approval of the supervisor, to ensure the work is examined on its own merit.

Examination without Oral Defense[1]

Not all doctoral programs have an oral examination, and some are examined by 'thesis only'.

Where the thesis undergoes an examination without oral defense, the exact process should be explained to the student. They should be clear about who will read the thesis, and how long the process will take. If the examiners request corrections or revisions, how these are to be done should be explained, and timescales given. It should be made clear to the student the point at which the thesis will be considered sustained. Where there is no oral defense, the examiners must still satisfy themselves about the same range of issues as if an oral examination had been conducted.

The Oral Examination

Where an oral examination takes place, it is a very important part of the process, and needs to be prepared for well. The reasons for holding an oral examination are essentially:

- Ensuring the thesis is the candidate's own work – they must be able to speak knowledgeably and in person about it. The oral examination thus stands as one of the safeguards against plagiarism in the thesis.
- The candidate demonstrates their ability to discuss and 'defend' academic work, which is a crucial dimension of academic discourse.

---

1. ICETE and the author recommend wherever possible that an oral defense should be part of the examination of the thesis.

- There is an opportunity to explain and express ideas further than just what is written on the page.
- The candidate can explain and justify the approach taken, and any questions that might arise.
- It allows a broader basis for examiner decisions than just the text.
- Ideas for publication or employment can follow.
- It generally works in the candidates favor – a borderline thesis can be helped by a good oral examination, but a poor thesis can't, although a student may be given more options for revisions if he/she defends it well.

The Examination Panel

This will vary from institution to institution based on the program itself. The supervisor should explain clearly to the student who is involved, and what role the supervisor will play. Normally an external examiner is part of the panel whose role is to bring objective assessment, and enable the work to be evaluated according to comparable standards in other leading institutions.

In some programs the student is consulted about choice of examiner. The supervisor should also play a role in recommending the most appropriate names, although final appointment is usually made by the institution itself. Key scholars in the field, those whose work the candidate has interacted with in their thesis, those who understand the context, are key people. They must be academic leaders in the subject area.

Setting the Examination Date

The institution usually finalizes the exam date, but the supervisor can prepare the way by liaising with the examiners and candidates to get a range of mutually convenient dates. This is not always easy at busy parts of the academic year. But the student should not be left waiting many months for the examination to be held.

In US-style PhD programs, as the dissertation committee size increases, so does the challenge of scheduling defense meetings. It is important that a Chair counsel the student to plan well ahead and explore possible defense dates without waiting to the last minute. In general, committee members will be very accommodating where they can be, but their schedules can be busy, making the scheduling of a defense difficult. An office assistant may be helpful in contacting the various members of the committee, exploring options for a defense meeting, and coordinating the planning of the event and its announcement within the school.

Preparing Students for Oral Examination

For many students, the oral defense of their doctoral thesis is a nightmare scenario. They view it as some form of relentless interrogation, perhaps imagining there will even be bright spotlights fixed on them, with examiners waiting to pounce on every slight mistake they make. The public defense which is central to the oral examination in some contexts, with a panel of experts debating the thesis before what can be a large audience of faculty, other students, and even the general public, can be a major ordeal. I have been involved in a number of doctoral examinations sometimes in the role of examiner, sometimes as an observer in the room but not participating, sometimes supporting students up to the moment the examination begins. The reality is rather different to the myth, and students need to be properly prepared with a good understanding of what might take place, and why it is a necessary part of the process in most doctoral systems.

A supervisor should always encourage doctoral students to see the examination as a positive thing:

- Here is an opportunity to talk in detail and at length about the topic that has been central to their life and thinking for the past few years.
- Some other scholars have actually read their thesis, and are interested in it!
- Here is a chance for the student to show just how much they know – there may be much more material that they did not put in the paper, and it will give them the opportunity to talk about their wider expertise.
- Here is a chance for the student show they are a world expert, and may even know the field better than their examiners.
- The thesis will be read by other experts who may make recommendations for corrections and revision which will improve it before publication.
- Examiners might make recommendations about publication of all or parts of the thesis. Important revisions can be suggested before the document is finalized, and goes into print. A nightmare oral thesis defense will only take place if the thesis is poor, and the candidate is not well prepared.

Preparing for the Day

Once the thesis has been submitted, the doctoral student should not stop working. They should continue to read, and refresh their thinking – new articles and books may come out subsequent to the submission date which they may be asked about.

Students need to learn to prepare for the oral examination just as they would for every other examination.

Helpful Exercises for Preparation

In readiness for the questions they will face, students can be asked to,

- Summarize the key theme of the thesis in a sentence – this is often a question examiners ask early on.
- Summarize in a few sentences the main points of argument in the thesis, and how one point builds from another with a logical structure.
- Summarize in a few sentences the unique contribution to knowledge they think the thesis makes.

Students need to also critically evaluate their own work, and see where it has been successful, and where it is less successful. It is useful to have a supervisory meeting before the examination in which you talk through issues that might come up in examination, and explore these and areas such as,

- The limitations of the thesis;
- Where further work is needed in the future;
- Where the research did not develop, turn out, in the ways expected.

Before the examination the student should,

- Carefully reread the thesis. They should look at each section and chapter and decide whether it stands up to the PhD quality test, and what questions examiners might ask about it.
- Learn to be their own examiner:

    i)   Is the thesis of the research clearly stated?

    ii) Does the thesis argument show awareness of the relevant literature?

    iii) Are the relevant sources cited properly?

    iv) Is the main argument coherent, logical, and well expressed?

    v)   Is there a clear line of development in the thesis throughout each paragraph, section, and chapter?

    vi) Where are the weak points in the thesis? Examiners are experienced at locating the areas where the argument is not strong.

    vii) Does the conclusion follow from the evidence collected?

The student can prepare some summary notes of the thesis in which they identify what are the key questions that they expect to be asked, then,

- Reduce its core contents to a few pages of notes;
- Provide explanations of the most complex part of the thesis;

- Learn short definitions of key terms and concepts used, so that they can speak confidently and knowledgeably about them;
- Show they are an expert on their own research;
- Be confident about their findings.

Explaining the Process

What will happen in the exam should be clearly explained to the student – often the exam process is shrouded in mystery – the most extraordinary rumors go round among students about what happens! Students need to know what is taking place, and to be able to practice the skills they need beforehand.

Where institutions have open defenses, allowing other students to attend, doctoral students should be encouraged or required to attend at least one other thesis defense prior to their own.

On the Examination Day

Students should ensure they are well rested before an oral exam – it is a very demanding process. As long as the preparatory steps above have been taken, the best option is a good night of sleep, rather than a final feverish reread of the thesis long into the night before.

The length of the examination can vary – one hour would be a short exam, two hours more normal, more than three hours is unusual.

Examination panels vary – from two examiners, to a large number of faculty and visiting examiner(s). This means approaches to questions can be very varied, and students need to be prepared for the different angles that might be taken.

Most doctoral programs allow a student to take a copy of their thesis into the examination, to which they can refer during the examination.

To make it easier to use, students can put colored paper inserts or marginal tabs to help them locate the chapters easily. This means they do not waste time fumbling about looking for sections. However, students are not normally allowed to take other papers or books into the exam apart from the thesis. A list of errata (spelling and typographical errors, grammatical issues, factual mistakes) which a student has identified after submission can be produced and shown to the examiners at the end of the exam if the student wishes to request permission to include these in the final revised version, but this should not include new sections of text.

Preparing to Meet the Examiners

The supervisor should help prepare the student for the time when they will meet those who will review the thesis in examination. The student may have been involved in discussions about choice of examiners, but they should also be prepared for the methodological and scholarly approaches the examiners may take, and questions they may pose.

The student should do some 'revision' about his examiners. If they have written in the area of the thesis, the student should read those texts, or reread them. They need to be aware of differences in approach and findings between their work and that of the examiners – and be able to explain and justify those differences.

If the student's work is interdisciplinary, they should be able to orientate examiners who are not subject specialists in their topic.

Preparing to Speak Well about the Thesis

Some institutions provide a pre-viva, or mock-viva experience. This can be helpful in preparing students for what is to come, giving them practice in answering questions they do not know about in advance, and hearing themselves provide answers. It takes time, and some students think it doubles the stress levels! If the supervisor is part of the examination panel, then the supervisor should not be part of a mock examination, but otherwise it can be helpful to be involved, or make suggestions for others who could help.

Students need to learn how to speak accurately and succinctly, with appropriate examples. Students must answer without rambling or 'waffling' by going away from the point, or introducing a lot a material that does not answer a question. Examiners get very frustrated when a student takes a long time answering a simple question. There are only so many questions that can be asked in the given time for the examination, and they want that time to be well spent. If a student does not know the answer to a question, it is best for them to say that, rather than talking round the topic for a long time without answering it.

Help the student to arrive looking interested, relaxed, enthusiastic (but not manically over enthusiastic!), willing to be open and self-critical about their work, and ready for a mature peer-level scholarly discussion.

The expected dress code should be explained to the student, so they do not have the embarrassment of arriving underdressed or overdressed.

Preparing for the Questions

If the supervisor is not part of the examination panel, based on your experience you can spend time working through what some of the likely questions the examiners will ask might be.

The first question is often an 'ice breaker' to relax the candidate. It might be something like, 'why did you choose to research this topic?' This may allow the student to talk about their personal motivation, but they also need to ensure they move on to answer with appropriate academic rigor – there should be a key research question in the field that needs an answer.

Students need to know what the likely questions might be, and to 'read' the question so that they understand the sort of skill they are being asked to speak about. Here are some examples:

i)   In a couple of sentences, what is your thesis? (Tthe student cannot answer, 'Oh, have you not read it then!')

ii)   What is the significance / original contribution of the thesis ? (going to the heart of the classic definition of research.)

iii) Do you think you covered all the issues indicated by your title? (which assesses the content.)

iv)   What were your research questions / hypotheses? (opening up the research methods used.)

v)   What other research approaches did you consider? Why did you choose this one? (again opening up the research methods used.)

vi)   If you were doing the research again, what would you do differently?

vii) Take us through your method using one of the sections of the thesis. Do you think your conclusions are justified? (the student needs to point exactly to where they have shown this.)

viii) How have you verified your findings? How does the conclusion hold together?

ix)   In what ways will scholarship need to change as a result of your thesis? (again original contribution.)

x)   Which of your findings surprised you most?

xi)   What do you think was your most important finding? (significance of the research.)

xii) What is the relevance or implications of the thesis for . . . ? (significance of the research.)

xiii) What further research issues grow out of your work?

xiv) How does your thesis compare with the work of . . . ? (requires you to be up-to-date on similar research and pertinent secondary literature.)

xv)   What is the greatest weakness in your approach? (self-criticism needs to be balanced with appropriate defense.)

xvi) How far are you satisfied with your research?

xvii) What will your next research work be on? (where does the thesis lead?)

Students also need to learn to answer using appropriate arguments, and where there is no clear answer, to say so. When examiners highlight inadequacies in the thesis, a student should defend their work where appropriate, but when the examiners clearly prove deficiencies or mistakes have been made, there is a need to back down and accept revisions are needed. Academic discourse and debate is appropriate, but having a heated argument with examiners is not! Nor is trying to defend the indefensible! Good scholars welcome critique, want to learn from it, and have their work improved by it.

Encourage the students to enjoy the experience as much as possible. It is an aspect of the rite of passage into their career as scholars, where they debate as serious academics at a peer level.

Preparing the Student for What Happens after the Oral Examination

The supervisor should go through the potential outcomes of the examination, so that the student knows exactly what the possibilities are and what may be required. If there are provisions for the examiners to require revisions, or corrections, what the nature of these might entail should be discussed, so the candidate is well prepared.

It has been my policy to be around on the day my students are examined. It is a stressful time for them, and they need support before and after. Some students will be elated by the result, others deeply disappointed. It can be hard for them to take in feedback or instructions given to them in the heat of the moment. Some are very emotionally vulnerable. Generally, arranging a celebration in advance is not the best policy. It is hard to deal with friends and family waiting with flowers, chocolates and preplanned celebrations if it has not gone well. Nothing is certain or predictable until the examiners have finished their work, otherwise there would be little need for the exam. Better to encourage them to wait until success is confirmed before arranging the party!

Further Reading

Lovitts, B. E. 'Making the Implicit Explicit.' In *The Assessment of Doctoral Education: Emerging Criteria and New Models for Improving Outcomes*, edited by P. L. Maki and N. A. Borkowski, 163–187. Sterling, VA: Stylus, 2006.

Murray, R. *How to Survive Your Viva: Defending a Thesis in an Oral Examination*. 2nd edition. Maidenhead: Open University Press, 2009.

Pearce, L. *How to Examine a Thesis*. Maidenhead: Open University Press, 2005.

Phillips, E. M., and D. S. Pugh. *How to Get a PhD: A Handbook for Students and Their Supervisors*. Maidenhead: Open University Press, 2010. (Kindle edition available also.)

Tinkler, P., and C. Jackson. *The Doctoral Examination Process: A Handbook for Students, Examiners and Supervisors*. Maidenhead: Open University Press, 2004 – based on the UK system, but with valuable principles.

Case Study

Lydia is a very bright student who writes well, and has clear research ability. You know she should write a thesis that will pass outright. However, she suffers badly from nervousness in public. One research presentation went badly wrong: she was so nervous she spoke very quickly and quietly and was almost inaudible to the audience. She ran over the time available and her presentation had to be stopped by the person chairing the meeting, and she ended up in tears. She has told you that when under stress her nervousness can make her physically sick.

Questions

How can you prepare Lydia for the examination of her thesis?

How can you help her be able to do oral presentations, which will be essential to the future academic career she hopes for?

17

Examining a Doctoral Thesis: Preparations before the Examination

To be invited to examine a doctoral thesis is a great honor. It means recognition of your status as a 'guardian of the discipline'. It also means great responsibility, and a very large amount of work. The way in which a doctoral examination is conducted, and the roles the examiners play, varies according to the program. The ICETE *Best Practice Guidelines* emphasize the need for examiners to be certain about the nature of their work before they begin the examination process:

> Examiners need to clearly understand the nature of their role within the doctoral examination process, and how final decisions about the granting of the academic award are arrived at. The institution needs to have clear guidelines and procedures in place for when there is a disagreement between examiners as to the result of a doctoral examination[1]

Reflective Questions

What was your own experience of doctoral examination?

What was the most helpful thing about it?

What was the least helpful thing about it?

What three things do you consider are the most important in examining a doctoral thesis?

---

1. Shaw, *Best Practice*, Section 20.

The Examiners

Institutions should ensure that examination panels for doctoral degrees are comprised of members with the skills that ensure a national and international equivalence of standards across the university / higher education sector. For this reason, institutions should have in place examination processes for doctoral degrees that normally include external examiner representation.[2]

Examiners must be properly qualified. They must be holders of a research doctoral award themselves, and be able to demonstrate research currency and activity. They should be chosen for their specialist knowledge of the subject area, the appropriate standards and benchmarks for the doctoral award, and should be active in research and doctoral supervision.

There is always some element of subjectivity in assessing written work, and working with a panel of examiners helps to counter that, but proper academic criterion and assessment should be used by all involved in the examinations process.

Those appointed external examiners need to have the required subject expertise, be scholars of international standing, be research-active and have major and current publications in the area being examined.[3]

One important issue is ensuring that the examination panel is made up not only of academic experts, but also of those who are subject specialists, and those who understand the approaches a student in an evangelical context may take. Examiners must be scrupulously fair, and mark good academic work highly even if they disagree with some of its theological content. However, unnecessary barriers should not be placed in a candidate's way by appointing examiners who are known to be hostile to a certain methodology taken, or theological approach. Nor should a special advantage be given to students by choosing examiners who may be overly sympathetic to the candidate's position. There should be proper academic rigor and balance among the examiners.

As the ICETE *Best Practice Guidelines* indicate:

Where doctoral examinations are conducted in evangelical academic contexts, the institution should ensure that examination panels are made up of members who have an understanding of the theological perspective of the institution and

---

2. Ibid., Section 21. An external examiner is someone who is not regularly employed by the institution where the doctoral research has been undertaken, and has not been involved in the supervision of the research student.

3. Shaw, *Best Practice*, Section 21, e.

the candidate, and an ability to ensure that the thesis / dissertation itself is examined purely on its academic merits.[4]

When asked to examine a thesis, the principle of academic integrity and fairness means the need to set aside personal preferences, and focus on the quality of the academic work presented.

Another important matter is the need to show proper academic ethics in declaring any personal interest in the candidate. If you are planning to employ the candidate, or planning to publish with the candidate, or if you have, or have had, any close personal or family relationship with the candidate, you should not normally be part of the examination panel.

Reflective Questions

What is the process in your institution for selecting examiners?

Who chooses them?

What materials are they provided with?

What training or induction are they given?

The External Examiner

To be asked to fulfil this role is an especial honor, and also a great responsibility. The external examiner (or reader) is someone from outside the institution who is selected to bring an outside measure of quality and objectivity – from a local university or seminary or from the global scholarly community. Their task is to ensure that a doctoral thesis would achieve a similar grade / award if it was submitted at doctoral level in a seminary or university somewhere else. Their role is to act especially as disinterested parties, and guardians of the discipline. In some institutions external readers act as advisors to the internal examiners by offering subject-specific comments about the thesis, without them formally acting as examiners. Usually external examiners / readers are part of an examination panel, and their role is to ensure a candidate examined is, according to external comparisons, not over-rewarded, or under-marked. The external examiner should receive payment from the institution conducting the examination. All arrangements relating to the appointment and payment of the examiners should be made by the institution.

---

4. Ibid.

The Supervisor on the Examination Panel

When the doctoral program allows the supervisor to be part of the examination panel, this allows opportunity to explain to the rest of the panel some of the work behind a thesis, and the reasons for approaches taken. However, there is an equal need for balance and objectivity. The work must be assessed on its academic merits, not on your personal feelings towards the candidate. There may be a temptation to 'get your student through' after many years of hard work together, but if the thesis is not of sufficient merit it should not pass. Similarly there is a temptation to become defensive if the work is criticized. It remains an assessment of the candidate's own work, and the panel is assessing that rather than the supervisor who has overseen it.

Reflective Questions

What are your feelings about being asked to be an examiner?

How have you ensured fairness and independent judgment when assessing work?

If you are an external examiner (reader), how can you best orientate yourself to the institution where you will examine and to the candidate's topic?

Preparing to Examine a Thesis

Before conducting a doctoral examination, a detailed process should be followed. Examiners should already be in mind when the student gives the institution formal notice to submit their thesis. This will save lengthy delays after submission while examiners are decided on and their availability ascertained. When the thesis is submitted they should be formally approached and appointed.

When deciding whether to accept an invitation to examine consider the following issues:

i)   Is the thesis on a subject at the heart of your research expertise? If it is not, the candidate will not get the best evaluation and feedback. Examining a thesis significantly outside your field of knowledge is not good practice.

ii)   Do you have the time to undertake the task? Done properly, an examination takes significant time – at least three or four days of your working time will be used up. Then there may be an oral examination event to attend, which may be held at some distance from your home. It is a great honor, and service to the wider academic community to do this, but recognize it is time consuming. Up to a week of your time will be used.

iii) Can you conduct the examination in reasonable time? It is unfair to keep candidates waiting many months until a suitable date can be found. In a rapidly changing scholarly field, research can become dated quickly. Also, the period of waiting can be extremely stressful for the candidate, and delay in holding an examination can mean they are unable to take up an academic post, or return to their home country.

iv) Are there any personal reasons why you should not examine – such as close relationship with the student?

What Examiners Do before an Examination

It is vital that the thesis is read very carefully! This may seem obvious, but I have known examinations where examiners did not appear to have close and detailed knowledge of the thesis, which is very bad practice. It is also unfair and disrespectful to the student.

It takes at least one or two full days to comprehensively read and evaluate an 80,000 word (350 page) thesis, and it should be read through at least twice.

The examiner needs to make detailed notes, comments, and prepare a list of possible questions. Relevant material, or other theses in this subject area, may need to be consulted. A good range of the references to other sources in the thesis should be checked for accuracy. Then a report will need to be produced, and lists of corrections that will be recommended produced. Doing such assessment and evaluation work thoroughly takes time, as does the examination itself.

Normally, the initial report is produced independently of the other examiners. This is submitted before meeting with the other examiners, to ensure an element of impartiality.

Programs with No Oral Examination

Doctoral programs which only examine the thesis give examiners no opportunity to meet with the candidate, and personal discussion and interaction is not possible. This has a number of advantages. It reduces costs, and tends to make the process quicker. It focuses the assessment on the thesis, which is the final product of the doctoral process, and is not distracted by a personal assessment of the candidate, only the work they have produced.

However, it does not allow the examiners to ascertain whether the thesis is the candidate's own work by asking them to meaningfully discuss it. Nor does it allow the examiners to probe more deeply, and ask questions behind what has been written. It does not allow the candidate to 'defend' or explain further their thinking in the thesis, nor engage in peer-level discussion with academic colleagues.

It is the recommendation of the ICETE *Best Practice Guidelines* that wherever possible an oral examination / thesis defense is held.

Programs with Oral Examination

The oral examination, or *viva voce* examination allows the examiners to ascertain whether the thesis is the candidate's own work by asking them to answer questions about it and meaningfully discuss what they have written. It proves an opportunity for examiners to probe more deeply to find the story behind what has been written, their choice of methods, and how the process worked, including challenges faced during the research process and changes of approach that were needed. It enables the candidate to 'defend' or explain further their thinking in the thesis, clarify certain points, and justify their approach and findings.

The oral examination allows a broader basis for examiner decisions to be taken than just the text. It enables the doctoral student to engage in peer-level academic discourse with scholarly colleagues, which is an important attribute of the doctoral graduate and marks their entry into the scholarly community of experts in the field.

There are some disadvantages to the oral examination. It can be a significant ordeal for candidates. It can penalize candidates who are nervous, or not good at oral presentation. Those who are being examined in a language that is not their own can be placed at a disadvantage. It brings a personal, and therefore more subjective, element into the examination that can sometimes work in the favor of the candidate and sometimes against. These factors can mitigate against the assessment being solely made on the basis of the work itself, and due allowance needs to be made for them.

When distance is a factor for examiners or candidates, it is possible for an examination to be conducted by telephone or electronic / video means, so long as the performance of the candidate is not prejudiced by use of these means. This is certainly less satisfactory than a face-to-face meeting, but practicalities sometimes dictate its necessity.

Reflective Questions

What sort of examination format does your doctoral program use?

What are its strengths and weaknesses?

The rest of this chapter focuses on the oral component of the examination which is the most common form, and is encouraged in the ICETE *Best Practice Guidelines*. Nonetheless, the principles that lie behind the approach that should be taken can be applied to programs without the oral examination.

Types of Oral Examination

Closed Room or Open Forum?

Even within the oral examination, across different doctoral programs there are great varieties.

In some situations, the examination is a private one, at which only the student, the examiners and a chairperson attend.

Sometimes the supervisor is a participant in the examination, in other systems they can only attend as an observer.

In a number of contexts the examination is a very public event, at which other academics, sometimes other students, family, friends, the general public attend.

If invited to examine a thesis it is important to understand what type of format the examination will take.

Celebration or Inquisition? – The Purpose of the Oral Examination

Again there are varieties across systems. In some cases the work of the examiner has largely been done before the oral examination takes place. The oral defense then becomes a public presentation of work undertaken, and celebration of achievement. The outcome is not in doubt.

In other contexts, although there has been a great deal of work done by the examiners before the oral defense, the decision of the examiners has not been made until the oral is over. The examination is just that, and during it the examiners must be convinced that the thesis written is of doctoral standard, that it is the candidates own work, and meriting the doctoral award. They should not announce their findings until they are clear that has been demonstrated.

Setting Up the Venue for the Oral Examination

If an oral examination is to be part of the examination process for the thesis, careful thought should be given as to the location and size of the venue. If the examination is a large public event, a lecture theatre, conference room, or large assembly hall is necessary. This should allow space for the audience, and the examiners and candidates need to be seen and heard clearly, without being crowded by the spectators. Microphones and audio equipment should be available and in good working order.

If the examination is not a public event, a small, more conducive venue is best – a tutorial room, seminar room, or office. Chairs should be arranged to allow ease of communication, and tables provided for the student and the examiners to put their papers and copies of the thesis on.

In all venues there should be essential equipment – a clock, water for the student and examiners, adequate ventilation, and a minimum of outside noise. All participants should be asked to switch cell phones off. A 'Do Not Disturb' sign on the door is a vital addition, to stop unnecessary interruptions.

And then you begin . . .

Case Study

Esther has been lecturing for a few years since completing her doctorate, and has supervised some masters student dissertations and marked them. Her Academic Dean approaches her to see if she is willing to act on the examining panel of one of the doctoral students in the department. The topic is in a field in which she has published two articles, so she has some expertise. Esther knows the student quite well, and they have had coffee together a couple of times. During the discussions the topic of the student's thesis has come up, and Esther has made a few suggestions about things to read. She is honored to be asked, but wonders if she can be truly impartial if she already knows the student. Also, she is very conscious of how recently she was a doctoral student herself, and does not feel very adequate to examine others.

Questions

Should Esther accept the invitation?

Is she sufficiently neutral and objective enough in this situation to take on the supervision because she knows the student?

How would you advise her about her feelings of inadequacy to take on this task?

Further Reading

Lovitts, B. E. 'Making the Implicit Explicit.' In *The Assessment of Doctoral Education: Emerging Criteria and New Models for Improving Outcomes*, edited by P. L. Maki and N. A. Borkowski, 163–187. Sterling, VA: Stylus, 2006.

Murray, R. *How to Survive Your Viva: Defending a Thesis in an Oral Examination*, 2nd edition. Maidenhead: Open University Press, 2009.

Pearce, L. *How to Examine a Thesis*. Maidenhead: Open University Press, 2005.

Tinkler, P., and C. Jackson. *The Doctoral Examination Process: A Handbook for Students, Examiners and Supervisors*. Maidenhead: Open University Press, 2004 – based on the UK system, but with valuable principles.

18

Examing the Thesis: The Examination Itself

For we must all appear before the judgment seat of Christ, that each one may receive what is due to him. (2 Cor 5:10)

Examine yourselves . . . test yourselves . . . and I trust that you will discover we have not failed the test. (2 Cor 13:5–6)

The principle of facing examination and assessment is something every Christian is aware of. The Scriptures make clear that we will be held to account for how we have lived and what we have done. We also know that the judge of all the earth will do right, and be absolutely fair in his examination, and in judgment justice will be applied with grace. Examiners of theses need to apply the same principles. Whether the thesis alone is examined, or whether it is supported by an oral defense, the task of the examiners remains the same. They must decide if the thesis meets the assessment criteria, or not. The examination should be conducted rigorously, fairly, justly, and with grace – a thesis will never be perfect.

Conducting the Oral Examination

At the outset, the examiners should explain to the student exactly what will happen in the exam. Students need to know what is taking place, and what they are going to be asked to do. The assessment procedures should be made clear beforehand, and they need to be operated rigorously, fairly and consistently. External members of an examination panel also need to understand exactly what the procedures are in the institution. Often an independent member of academic faculty chairs the examination to ensure due process.

Length

There is no set length for an oral examination. An examination of less than an hour does not give much time for in-depth analysis. If the length is over three hours it can become a significant ordeal for the student, and most ground should have been covered before that length of time has elapsed. Somewhere around two hours is more normal.

An examiner will find that together with the preparatory meeting, the examination itself, and the discussions and report writing afterwards, the whole process takes up at least half of a day. This is in addition to the several days spent reading and evaluating the thesis beforehand.

Questions

Examiners should meet before the examination starts to discuss the list of questions they would like the candidate to answer, and allocate them to different members of the panel. There should be a variety of questions covering issues across the thesis, and no one examiner should dominate the questioning, although the external examiner should play the prominent role.

Reflective Questions

What would be a good 'ice breaker' question to begin an oral examination with?

What sort of questions can be used to explore whether the candidate has properly identified a question / problem that lies behind the thesis?

How would you get a candidate to talk about their methodology?

What do you do if a candidate can't answer a question you ask, which you feel they should be able to answer?

What sort of questions can you ask to ensure the work is the candidate's own?

What questions can be used to explore whether a thesis is an 'original contribution to knowledge'?

Key Issues in Questioning

- It is important to allow the candidates to speak and express in their own words the heart of the thesis. However, it is important to keep them focused on answering the question.

- If a student is speaking at length without answering a question they should be challenged about this.
- Students should have opportunity to 'defend' the thesis.
- Questions should be clearly expressed and penetrating, but they should not be hostile. The purpose is to develop a peer-level, respectful academic discussion.
- Students should be made to think, and questions should be challenging, but it is not fair to subject them to a relentless 'grilling.'
- The role of the chairperson of the examination is important, and they should intervene if they feel the tone is unhelpful, or the candidate is being treated unfairly.

Examining the Thesis

The key question to ask is, what doctoral-level qualities must the examiners find have been demonstrated in the thesis in order to consider it sustained and to pass?

These issues apply whether the thesis is examined by text only, or with an oral examination. In the context of a doctoral examination in an evangelical theological institution, the *ICETE Beirut Benchmarks*[1] set out the qualities a successful doctoral candidate must demonstrate. It will be helpful to use these as a form of checklist to assess the attainments of the candidate.

These skills are:

> **Beirut Benchmark 1: Comprehensive understanding,** *having demonstrated a breadth of systematic understanding of a field of study relevant to the Christian community of faith, and mastery of the skills and methods of research appropriate to that field.*

The examiners need to be convinced that the student has understanding that is 'deep and systematic'. What questions can be used to enable a student to demonstrate that their understanding of their research field matches this criterion?

What in a thesis does an examiner look for to demonstrate whether a student is a 'master of the skills and methods of research appropriate to that field'?

In an evangelical context, it is appropriate to explore the relevance of the research and its conclusions to the Christian community of faith. What questions can be used by the examiner in order to do this?

> **Beirut Benchmark 2: Critical skills, faithfully exercised**, *having demonstrated their capacity for critical analysis, independent evaluation of primary and secondary source materials, and synthesis of new and inter-related*

---

1. 'Beirut Benchmarks,' in *Best Practice*, ed. I. Shaw.

ideas through coherent argumentation, and their commitment to exercise such skills on the foundation of biblical faithfulness to Jesus Christ and his church.

In what ways can you assess the high-grade academic skills of critical analysis, independent evaluation, synthesis, and coherent argumentation?

What aspects of a candidate's work indicate that they are able to write with academic integrity and rigor, and demonstrate ability to do this consistently within their faith perspective?

> **Beirut Benchmark 3: Serious inquiry with integrity,** *having demonstrated the ability to conceive, design and implement a substantial project of inquiry and to do so with Christian and scholarly integrity, resulting in a sustained and coherent thesis.*

This takes the examiner to the heart of assessing the research abilities of the candidates and the methods they have used. The ability to 'conceive' a project, and then carry it through to completion, is central to their future life as a scholarly teacher and researcher. The examiner must judge how effectively this has been done.

Are the research methods appropriate, and consistently applied? The student should show the ability to make informed judgments in complex fields. In essence the doctoral thesis has to demonstrate that the student has become an accepted expert in their field. After gaining a doctorate they should be able to go on and undertake their own research in an independent, self-managed, and self-sustaining way without the support of a supervisor. The ability to develop and adapt research to deal with unexpected evidence or outcomes is the mark of scholarly research.

The word 'integrity' highlights the need for consistency between scholarship and Christian profession. If such consistency is lacking, as when plagiarism is detected, or sources have not been treated fairly or truthfully, it is a failure of both Christian and scholarly integrity. The examiners need to explore this area carefully in all cases.

What type of questions in the oral examination will allow all these areas to be explored?

> **Beirut Benchmark 4: Creative and original contribution,** *having produced, as a result of such disciplined inquiry, a creative and original contribution that extends the frontiers of knowledge, or develops fresh insights in the articulation and contextual relevance of the Christian tradition, some of which merit national or international refereed publication.*

The thesis needs to show the candidate has strong abilities in the 'creation and interpretation' of knowledge – this takes us into the area of 'originality' which is the hallmark of the doctoral thesis.

Are the research findings a product of the student's own work? The *Benchmarks* speak of both extending 'the frontiers of knowledge', but also of bringing 'fresh insights'. The research field does not need to be entirely new – indeed in areas of biblical studies and theology much of the subject matter will have been well worked over, but 'fresh insights' allows for new perspectives, new interpretations, of existing material to be seen as original.

An external benchmark is also noted – the work should merit 'national or international refereed publication'. If the thesis marks the passage of the researcher into the scholarly community, this is the accepted standard of entrance, and the level they should be judged capable of working at hereafter. Examiners will often recommend ways of having a thesis, or parts of it, published at the end of the examination.

The examiners must benchmark the work as being at the 'D' level – doctoral academic level – and being at the 'forefront of academic discipline'. That is the reason why an examination panel must include qualified examiners who are themselves research-active. Through the examination the guardians of the discipline need to determine whether the student has reached the appropriate level to conduct research independently and be qualified to supervise others at doctoral level.

> **Beirut Benchmark 5: Contextual relevance,** *having shown their capacity, in the course of their doctoral program and in their expectation of its future potential, for biblically-informed critical engagement with the realities of their cultural contexts.*

This is particularly important for research undertaken in an evangelical theological context. The candidate should be able to express the reason for which their research was undertaken, and its potential relevance for the context it dealt with, or which they will work in.

Again, examiners in evangelical institutions are looking for integration of academic ability and scriptural foundations in the 'biblically-informed critical engagement' with context.

> **Beirut Benchmark 6: Ability to communicate,** *having shown an ability in communicating about their area of expertise to peer-level academic audiences, and, where appropriate, to non-specialists in local Christian communities and the wider society in culturally relevant ways, including their mother tongue, for example through teaching, preaching or writing.*

The examiners need to ascertain whether the candidate has the 'ability to communicate ideas to peer-level academic audiences and non-specialist audiences'. The academic audience is obviously the examiners themselves, although the student may also go on into a teaching career so they need to show communication ability conducive to that.

The 'non-specialist audience' requirement is to ensure the research findings are disseminated as widely as possible, rather than just within the narrow confines of the academic community. How will these ideas change thinking, or confirm thinking in the wider context, churches, or of Christian leaders, as well as in the scholarly discipline. Asking a student to describe how they would explain their work to a non-specialist in their church or a person sitting on a bus, is one way of testing this skill. This is not just testing basic communication skills, but also reveals something much deeper. As Albert Einstein is supposed to have said, 'If you can't explain it simply you don't understand it well enough.' In order to explain simply you must understand profoundly.

It is obviously difficult to assess ability to teach or preach during a two or three hour examination setting, and these aspects of a student's development should, where appropriate, be assessed throughout their course by other means, and become a part of the holistic skills development that the program seeks – as set out in chapter 15.

> **Beirut Benchmark 7: Missional impact,** *having shown that they are committed, and can be expected, to use the fruit of their doctoral study, the skills it has given them and the opportunities it affords them, to promote the kingdom of God and advance the mission of the church (both local and global), through transformational service and Christ-like leadership, to the glory of God.*

This opens up the area of the long-term outcomes of doctoral study, and questions of what skills the student has developed during doctoral study.

- Do they show signs of the ability to relate the academic skills they have developed to a missional purpose, and promoting the kingdom of God?
- Is the project publishable? Has the candidate thought through ways it will advance the mission of the church?
- Are the materials produced capable of opening up broader discussion in different but related topics?
- Does the student understand the implications for their research, in this, and other related fields and in their church contexts?
- What further research will flow from the project, and how might that promote the kingdom of God? It is good for examiners during an oral examination to explore to see what lies 'beneath the iceberg'. Does the candidate have a great deal more research material that they have not used, and if so how will they use it in further research or writing projects?
- What potential as a future researcher do they show?
- Does the candidate show evidence of skills in teaching? In time the student may become a teacher of others, or a supervisor of other doctoral students, using the skills they have gained. Examiners are sometimes asked to act as referees

when students they have examined apply for a job, or to recommend them for suitable posts, so it is good to assess how they communicate key concepts and information during the examination process.

The Result

The Beirut Benchmarks cover the overall attainments to be demonstrated in the doctoral thesis and its examination. Across these key Benchmarks there will be some variation in ability demonstrated, and what examiners are looking at is a good overall score. So a thesis may demonstrate excellence in all the Benchmarks, but not be communicated very well orally during the defense. Such a candidate would be unlikely to be failed. But, similarly, if a thesis was brilliantly communicated, but was weak in all the other Benchmarks, it would not pass, and major revision would be required.

So, what are the potential results?

Generally, a range of academic outcomes are available to the examiners, but this will vary according to the institution. Also some systems have a simple pass or fail with no levels demarcated, others have a range of grades within the pass – such as *Cum Laudae*, or *Magna Cum Laudae*.

Depending on the system, these are some of the possible award outcomes:

- Straight award of the thesis (sometimes with a grade).
- Award subject to minor corrections.
- Award subject to significant revisions and rewriting (without re-examination).
- Major revision and resubmission with a second oral examination.
- Award of a lower degree (e.g. MPhil).
- No degree awarded.

These should be communicated clearly and efficiently to the student, with appropriate explanations.

Where examination results are confirmed by a higher degrees committee within the institution, any decision communicated by the examining panel is normally only provisional. Usually the examiners can only indicate that they are recommending the candidate for a certain award. The degree is generally formally conferred by the highest academic body in the institution, or an external validating body.

Institutions must have in place clear policies concerning the relationship between the examining board, and the higher body that confirms the award, and regulations for resolving any disputes. Institutions need to ensure that these processes operate smoothly, and final award decisions are quickly communicated to the candidate.

Communication of Results to the Student and Supervisor

Because of the significant investment of intellectual and emotional energy expended by the candidate when there is an oral examination, students can find difficulty in fully hearing and understanding the result communicated to them at the end of the examination. The outcome achieved and what it means (especially if further revisions or corrections are needed) should be explained carefully to the student.

Oral feedback should be followed by written feedback and detailed instructions sent to the candidate within a few days of the examination to enable revisions to be quickly undertaken.

Students should be encouraged to see that being given corrections and amendments is to ensure the work fits with the academic level and criteria. The thesis will need to take its place in the academic literature at the right level, and it should be stressed the final and permanent copy of the thesis which is submitted after revision will need to be available for inspection. Students will want to ensure it is of the highest possible quality.

Usually the supervisor / chair of the dissertation committee of the candidate helps support the candidate in the process of making the revisions necessary. It is important that all corrections and revisions stipulated by examiners are completed before a pass is sustained. Usually a member of the examination panel from the candidate's institution has this responsibility, but if the external examiner makes special recommendations he/she may have responsibility to ensure they are completed. If a thesis is to be published a thorough spelling and grammar check should be undertaken before it is made available for publication.

A Checklist of Key Issues for Examiners to Consider

i) Does the thesis make a distinct and original contribution to knowledge?
- Is the candidate now able to conduct independent research?

ii) Has the candidate got a good knowledge of the field?
- Do the bibliography and the references reflect the current state of scholarship?
- Does the student understand the extent and the limits of his/her contribution?
- Has the candidate genuinely shown a mastery of the key literature, and shown where their contribution fits in with it?
- Has the candidate made connections between the review of literature, and the rest of their study – showing how their study arises from issues, or gaps, in the wider academic debate?

- Does the candidate make connections between their research findings and the key scholarly literature throughout the whole of their thesis, to show how their work takes the debate on, or changes the field?

iii) Is the thesis a piece of original work?
- Has the student demonstrated that they did the work?
- Did the student write the entire thesis?
- What will you do if you suspect plagiarism of part of the content?
- Is the candidate aware of their own self-positioning with regard to the research topic?
- In what way does the content, methods, findings, proposals for the future demonstrate 'originality'.

iv) Have the appropriate methods been used and understood?
- Have the proper procedures in research ethics been followed?
- Is the student aware of the limits to the reliability of these methods?
- Are the methods valid for this study?
- What was the rationale for the choice of texts / sources used?
- Can appropriate conclusions be extrapolated by using these methods?

v) Is there a clear thread of logical argument in the thesis?
- Do the main chapters build out of the introduction, and connect to the literature review?
- Do the chapters connect together, and flow in proper sequence?
- Are the key directions in each chapter set out at the start and conclusions given at the end?
- Does the conclusion build out of the thesis, and bring the different aspects of the debate in the chapters together in one place? Does it answer the research questions posed in the introduction?
- Does the conclusion conclude the work, or is new material and new argument that goes in other directions suddenly introduced?
- Does everything in the conclusion properly belong there?

vi) Is the literary style and standard of presentation suitable for a doctoral thesis that should be capable of international academic publication?

vii) Is the whole or part of the thesis worthy of publication?

viii) Did the candidate explain and present work well in the oral examination?
- Is the student able to defend the work and the thesis confidently when in discussion with her/his academic peers?

Problem Areas

Institutions must have in place clear policies concerning the relationship between the examining board, and the higher body that confirms the award, and regulations for resolving any disputes.[2]

Split Decisions

Because examiners bring an element of subjectivity to the examining process, they do not always agree on an outcome. Where examiners are split in their decision, the institutional regulations should outline the procedure that is to be followed.

Is a majority verdict possible? What happens if the external examiner is in a minority? Does he or she have a casting vote?

In some institutions, if examiners are unable to agree on a decision, there is provision to constitute a new examination panel, and for the thesis to be re-examined.

The Student Complains about the Result

Again the institutional regulations should have clear guidance on what grounds a student can appeal, and the proper process that should be followed in all cases.

The presence of an independent chair for the examination can help alleviate the grounds for some potential complaints. It is the chairperson's duty to make sure that the candidate is treated fairly, and proper process is followed. They should also ensure the creation and processing of proper records and reports, which are initially independently created by the examiners.

Generally the student cannot complain about inadequate supervision as a cause of their academic failure after the thesis has been examined. All such complaints should be lodged before the examination, and appropriate action and measures put in place. This needs to be regularly communicated to the student by the institution. Some students may hesitate to complain out of fear of adverse consequences on their continuation in the program and graduation. This is an important matter that needs careful attention, and needs to be explained clearly to the student. It is important that they have the best possible experience throughout the duration of their program, rather than problems emerging at the end of the period of study when it is too late and they have adversely affected the outcome. The operation of regular and robust feedback mechanisms should also prevent problems persisting unnoticed.

---

2. Shaw, *Best Practice*, Section 13, f.

Into the Future

It is common for examiners to be asked to support the student in the outworking of their future academic career. They might be asked to provide references for jobs. Examiners often recommend ways a thesis can be published. This is all appropriate once the examination is finished, and the thesis pass confirmed. In a sense, the examiners work is never fully over in these circumstances, but it is a great privilege to welcome and help integrate the holder of a newly awarded doctorate into the scholarly community, and watch with interest their development as a research scholar. One day they may even ask you to examine one of their own doctoral students!

Reflective Questions

If you are new to examining, what are the three most important pieces of information you need to ask from the institution before examining a PhD thesis?

Who can you ask about these?

If you are an experienced examiner, what three lessons would you want to share with your less-experienced academic colleagues about the process of doctoral examination?

Case Study

John is new to examining. The first thesis he is on the exam panel for is one that interests him, and he has done work in this field, However, he feels the thesis is quite weak in key areas of knowledge and method, and expects the other examiners to agree, He is surprised to hear that most of the comments from the others are positive, and they see no problem in awarding a pass. The external examiner is also positive, although John realizes that the thesis is not really in the external examiners core area.

Questions

What institutional issues does this raise?

What should John do?

What do you do if you strongly disagree with the other examiners in a doctoral examination?

Further Reading

Lovitts, B. E. 'Making the Implicit Explicit.' In *The Assessment of Doctoral Education: Emerging Criteria and New Models for Improving Outcomes*, edited by P. L. Maki and N. A. Borkowski, 163–187. Sterling, VA: Stylus, 2006.

Pearce, L. *How to Examine a Thesis*. Maidenhead: Open University Press, 2005.

Tinkler, P., and C. Jackson. *The Doctoral Examination Process: A Handbook for Students, Examiners and Supervisors*. Maidenhead: Open University Press, 2004.

Conclusion

This handbook has sought to demonstrate that supervising doctoral students is a great privilege, a great responsibility, and also a very significant opportunity to invest in the training of some of the most strategic current and future Christian leaders. It is certainly a learning process. Some doctoral students prove a tremendous blessing to work with, but others can disappoint us and they don't achieve all we hoped for. However, it is best not to judge the value of the investment of time on the experience of supervising just one or two students, but take the longer view.

Each student supervised will take an investment of several hundred hours of work, yet in terms of 'value-added', training doctoral students scores very highly. Doctoral supervision involves facilitating the extension of biblical and theological knowledge and awareness, and working to develop cutting-edge responses to some of the most important issues facing the church today. It also ensures students develop skills in research and writing to the highest standards, which will benefit the church for many years to come. Doctoral students often become theological educators, so investing time in their training involves working with those who will train future preachers, teachers and Christian leaders.

The supervision of doctoral students also has implications far beyond the local context. In today's globalized environment, the PhD can never be an isolated and local academic program. Through working with doctoral students the supervisor is contributing to the fostering of international cooperation, and collaboration, which can break down barriers and be a force for strengthening partnership within global theological education. As such it is a vital resource for both the local and the global church.

This handbook has encouraged reflection on practice, enhancing the good work already being done, and fostering change where it is needed. The supervisor should always be open to new learning and approaches, responding to student needs, adapting to changing circumstances and opportunities. The handbook has sought to apply a series of key principles, also found in the ICETE *Best Practice Guidelines for Doctoral Programs,* to the work of the evangelical supervisors.

- Supervision in evangelical theological contexts involves more than developing academic skills, but also requires investing in the spiritual formation of those supervised. There should be close integration between academic and spiritual formation in how supervision is done, and what is expected of the student. The spiritual formation desired rests on the conviction that the Bible is foundational to belief and practice. Doctoral supervisors should foster the biblically-informed integration of learning and living. All aspects of the supervisory relationship should reflect the highest standards of ethical and moral integrity and demonstrate consistency in striving for academic and spiritual excellence.

- Doctoral supervisors in theological disciplines should take a missional approach their task. Doctoral students need to be equipped with a breadth of knowledge, understanding, and critical thinking skills to enable them to be leaders of theological education in the future, and to do this with a global perspective. The missional purpose of doctoral education in theological disciplines means that the doctorate should not be seen as an end in itself, but as a way of serving the church through training trainers – those who will prepare the next generation of preachers, pastors, teachers, and Christian leaders. The skills built through doctoral education should also be those that will help sustain a future ministry of teaching, research and writing in theological education and leadership.

- The doctoral supervisor should work to break down the disconnection between the academy and the local church, especially as it occurs at the higher levels of study. He or she should model active commitment to the local church as the expression of the body of Christ, and encourage similar commitment on the part of the student.

- Doctoral studies should be done in community. Both supervisor and student should play a full and active role in the spiritual and academic dimensions of this. The training offered should also facilitate collaboration with brothers and sisters in Christ in the global academic community, building international networks and partnerships, in the work of theological education as an aspect of the mission of God.

- Doctoral supervisors should encourage research that is relevant to context. There should be a commitment by supervisors to serve the church by supporting PhD students who are not only academically excellent but who have the skills that are most needed in their context, and who address topics designed to solve the key theological, and social, and missiological challenges that the church faces.

- Doctoral supervisors should ensure that students are fully able to engage both with global academic discourse, and the global nature of the church. Students should be encouraged to play a full part in the global theological enterprise, and where possible spend part of their period of study in another context or culture. Supervisors should also play their role in promoting and serving theological education in diverse contexts and cultures. Supervisors should therefore be committed to training 'world theologians' – who contribute to the world church, while understanding the global dynamics and implications of their subject for their local context. They should also bring the riches of that local context into global theological discourse.

This partnership should work so as to reduce the so called 'brain drain' of the best theological minds from the Majority World to the West, and intentionally work to challenge inequality in the global distribution of theological resources. This involves a commitment to sharing information, data, and resources.

Doctoral supervisors should play a full role in creating a research culture, which involves a supportive institutional environment in which doctoral students can flourish. This means facilitating students accessing the best academic resources, and also creating an ideas culture where creative thinking can be nurtured in a godly fashion, clearly articulated, tested against Scripture, evaluated against the best in contemporary scholarship, and relevantly applied.

- Supervisors should model good practice in team working and collaboration in supervision. While retaining a strong emphasis on their core disciplines, supervisors should demonstrate openness to interdisciplinary approaches where it serves the project of the student.
- Evangelical doctoral supervisors should be committed to the application of international standards of quality assurance and excellence in doctoral education. They should take their full part in the debates on theological education towards achieving international consensus on what doctoral education is, the skills required, and the outcomes expected. The supervisor should model academic excellence and inculcate it in those they supervise.
- Doctoral supervisors must promote well-functioning academic structures. There must be a commitment by supervisors to achieving strong effectiveness indicators – such as high completion rates, short time to degree, high levels of employability, commitment to service to church.
- When working as examiners supervisors must ensure that the assessment and examination of doctoral degrees is rigorous and appropriate to the highest level of academic work.

I pray that global evangelical theological education is enhanced through the readers of this handbook taking on applying these key principles and the range of other advice and suggestions it contains.

I look forward with anticipation in coming years to reading the key contributions to global evangelical theological discourse that your students will produce!

Appendix 1

Annual Doctoral Student Feedback Form

Date _____

1. Supervisory meetings with my main supervisor / dissertation committee chair have been sufficiently frequent.

1	2	3	4	5

Strongly Agree   Strongly Disagree

How frequently have you met or had contact with your supervisor?

Comment on the appropriateness of this?

2. My main supervisor / dissertation chair has been available for informal contact outside formal supervision meetings.

1	2	3	4	5

Strongly Agree   Strongly Disagree

Comments:

3. The advice and support I have been given by my main supervisor / dissertation chair has been satisfactory.

1	2	3	4	5

Strongly Agree   Strongly Disagree

Comments:

4. The advice and support I have been given by my second supervisor / reader has been satisfactory.

1	2	3	4	5

Strongly Agree   Strongly Disagree

How often have you met with your second supervisor / reader?

Comment on the appropriateness of this.

Other comments.

5. The induction and continuing training program for postgraduate research has been satisfactory.

1	2	3	4	5

Strongly Agree   Strongly Disagree

What opportunities were you offered?

What did you take advantage of?

Comments:

6. The administrative help and support in the process of application, registration, and financial requirements has been satisfactory.

1	2	3	4	5

Strongly Agree   Strongly Disagree

Comments:

7. The library has provided appropriate resources for postgraduate research, including obtaining access to other institutions where appropriate.

1	2	3	4	5

Strongly Agree   Strongly Disagree

Comments:

8. The Research Seminar has proved helpful in fostering a research community, and stimulating thinking.

1	2	3	4	5

Strongly Agree   Strongly Disagree

Comments:

9. If you have delivered a paper at the Research Seminar, how did it help with developing your research thinking and skills? (Otherwise write not applicable)

1	2	3	4	5

Strongly Agree   Strongly Disagree

Comments:

10. The doctoral program has allowed adequate opportunities for integration with community life.

1	2	3	4	5

Strongly Agree   Strongly Disagree

Comments:

11. My supervisors and the study institution have given appropriate support for pastoral care and spiritual formation.

1	2	3	4	5

Strongly Agree   Strongly Disagree

Comments:

12. The institution has provided an appropriate learning environment for research, and developing future skills for future ministry in academic teaching and writing.

1	2	3	4	5

Strongly Agree   Strongly Disagree

Comments:

13. I am overall satisfied with the research experience that has made available to me.

1	2	3	4	5

Strongly Agree   Strongly Disagree

Comments:

Please write below any other comments on how the institution can improve or develop its support for postgraduate students.

Appendix 2

Student Feedback Form on Completion of Doctorate

Instructions: Please respond to the following questions and share with us as well as you can your assessment of your experience as a dissertation student in our doctoral program. Your responses to these questions will be anonymous; so do not include any information in your responses that would identify you or your dissertation topic. Thanks for your help with this survey!

Availability of Supervisor and Readers

Given that faculty members have a range of responsibilities in their roles in the doctoral program (e.g. dissertation supervision, teaching, grading, advising, administration, research and writing):

1. In general, how well do you feel that your first supervisor / dissertation chair made himself/herself available to you to discuss your dissertation plans and work? (Circle one)

5	4	3	2	1
Always	Almost Always	Generally	Sometimes	Rarely

If you experienced a problem in this area, what was it?

2. In general, how well do you feel that your second and third supervisors / readers made themselves available to you to discuss your dissertation plans and work? (Circle one)

5	4	3	2	1
Always	Almost Always	Generally	Sometimes	Rarely

If you experienced a problem in this area, what was it?

Profitability of Time When Meeting

3. When you did meet with your supervisor / dissertation chair, did you find that the interaction you had was beneficial to your understanding how to go about the aspects of your work that you were meeting to discuss? (Circle one)

5	4	3	2	1
Always	Almost Always	Generally	Sometimes	Rarely

If you experienced a problem in this area, what was it?

4. When you did meet with your second or third supervisors / readers, did you find that the interaction you had was beneficial to your understanding how to go about the aspects of your work that you were meeting to discuss? (Circle one)

5	4	3	2	1
Always	Almost Always	Generally	Sometimes	Rarely

If you experienced a problem in this area, what was it?

Practical Guidance

5. As you know, the thesis / dissertation requires different kinds of work at different stages of the process. In reflecting back on your experience with your dissertation committee, please evaluate how helpful they were in giving you feedback and guidance in successfully navigating these aspects of the dissertation. Use this scale in your responses: (Circle one for each)

	Very Helpful	Mostly Helpful	Somewhat Helpful	Not Very Helpful
Focusing the topic	4	3	2	1
Literature review	4	3	2	1
Theological integration work	4	3	2	1
Planning the research approach and methods	4	3	2	1

Data analysis	4	3	2	1
Conclusions, implications	4	3	2	1
Supporting documents (Appendices, etc.)	4	3	2	1

For any areas where you experienced a significant problem, please provide us with a brief description:

Timely Feedback

In our program, we tell students that when they submit a document to a committee member, they should allow up to two weeks for the faculty member to review the material and send their feedback.

6. What characterized your experience of receiving feedback from your supervisor / dissertation chair? (Circle one)

5	4	3	2	1
Always on time	Almost always on time	Generally on time	Sometimes on time	Rarely on time

7. In this same area, what characterized your experience with your second and third supervisors / readers? (Circle one)

5	4	3	2	1
Always on time	Almost always on time	Generally on time	Sometimes on time	Rarely on time

Encouragement and Support

8. How would you describe the quality of encouragement and support your supervisor / dissertation chair provided throughout the dissertation process? (Circle one)

5	4	3	2	1
Excellent	Good	Fair	Weak	Poor

If you experienced a problem in this area, what was it?

9. How would you describe the quality of encouragement and support your second and third supervisors / readers provided throughout the dissertation process? (Circle one)

5	4	3	2	1
Excellent	Good	Fair	Weak	Poor

If you experienced a problem in this area, what was it?

Preparation for Defense

10. When the time came to prepare for your proposal defense, and/or your dissertation defense, did you receive adequate advice from your supervisor / dissertation chair on how to prepare for the defense? (Circle one)

5	4	3	2	1
Excellent	Good	Fair	Weak	Poor

If you experienced a problem in this area, what was it?

Follow Up after the Final Defense

Following the final thesis / dissertation defense, there is generally additional revision work to do.

11. Did you receive adequate guidance from your supervisor / dissertation chair on making the final revisions needed so the dissertation could then be approved. (Circle one)

5	4	3	2	1
Excellent	Good	Fair	Weak	Poor

If you experienced a problem in this area, what was it?

Final Questions

12. Given your experience in your research work, if you were getting started on your thesis /dissertation now, would you want to work with the same supervisor / dissertation committee chair and supervisory team / committee members? (Circle one)

3	2	1
Yes	No	I'm not sure

If you answered "Yes," what stands out as the primary reasons why you would want the same supervisors / committee members?

If you answered "No," what stands out as the primary reasons why you would want at least some different dissertation committee members?

If you answered "I'm not sure," what are the main issues that cause you to be uncertain about this?

13. Knowing that various students may respond differently to the dissertation / thesis supervision approaches and processes of a particular doctoral faculty member, what kind of student do you think would benefit most from the approaches your dissertation chair took with you?

Thanks for taking the time to respond to these questions, helping us do our best in the dissertation / thesis supervision process.

Appendix 3

Research Student Progression Checklist

1. Research Methods and Skills Training

Form of training _____

Topics covered _____

Way assessed _____

Areas for further training in next twelve months _____

Point at which key skills considered as attained _____

2. Thesis / Dissertation Proposal

Initial draft _____

Full draft _____

Date formally approved _____

3. Specific Language Requirements

Courses taken _____

Further courses required _____

Further languages considered desirable _____

Appropriate language competence confirmed _____

4. Christian Ministry Opportunities

In what ways has the doctoral student maintained involvement in other aspects of Christian ministry and service over the past twelve months?

In what ways has the doctoral student maintained involvement in other aspects of Christian ministry and service over the duration of their doctoral studies?

In what ways have the student and supervisor reflected on these, and their integration into the study profile?

What key issues have arisen?

Are student and supervisor satisfied these are appropriate for the stage of academic progress currently reached, and that they do not impinge on study time?

5. Local Church Life

Has the student demonstrated consistent involvement in the life and witness of a local church?

Location: _____
Level of involvement: _____

Lessons learned for integration of faith and scholarship:

6. Attendance at Community Worship Events within the Institution

Has the student demonstrated consistent involvement in times when the study institution meets as a worshiping community?

Note any issues or challenges that have arisen.

What changes and developments have been agreed for the next twelve months?

7. Engagement with Institutional Learning Community

Has the student demonstrated evidence of active engagement in the institution's learning community? This includes:

Regular attendance at Research Seminars and formal academic lectures, including those given by visiting scholars.

Participation in discussion and debate in seminars, demonstrating engaged listening, informed questioning, handling disagreements with grace, working as a team with others.

8. Presentation of Seminar

Has the student made a formal presentation at an academic seminar in the past year?

Did they demonstrate the following skills?

i)   Ability to communicate complex material and concepts in accessible and interesting ways.

ii)   Capacity to respond to questions in an informed and relevant manner.

iii)   Ability to maintain justifiable views in the face of questioning and challenge, but also to change views where appropriate.

iv)   Ability to handle criticism with grace.

Has formal feedback been given to the student on their seminar presentation, and if so what were the key points of that?

What are the plans for the next twelve months?

9. Theological Awareness

What key theological issues have been discussed as areas for increased attention and growth over the past year?

What further areas need to be considered?

Have any specific 'problem areas' been raised, and have these been satisfactorily been addressed by student and supervisor?

Can the student explain how their doctoral program has been shaping his/her theological perspectives over the past year?

10. Teaching Practice

What opportunities were taken to gain teaching experience?

Lectures given _____

Seminars given _____

Tutorials led _____

Online teaching opportunities _____

What opportunities has the student had to design and grade different forms of student assessment?

Supervisor Feedback on Teaching Experience

How effective was the student at communication of key course material at an appropriate level to students?

To what degree did the student demonstrate effectiveness in using a variety of communication methods and technologies?

Was the feedback given to student learning appropriate?

What are the goals for the next twelve months?

11. Integration with Wider Academic Community

Academic conferences attended in past year _____

Presentation of research at an academic conference or meeting of professional society

Meeting: _____

Title of presentation: _____

Academic material (book review, article, etc.) accepted for publication
_____

What are the plans for the next twelve months in this area?

12. Doctoral Examination

Discussion of potential examiners, including external expert _____

Appointment of examining panel _____

Examination of doctoral thesis _____

Thesis revisions completed _____

Recommendations for publication made _____

13. Continuous Professional Development

Have the student and doctoral supervisor discussed ways to ensure continuous professional development post-doctorate for the student, and furtherance of research activities.

Outline plan years 1–2 _____

Outline plan years 3–4 _____

Outline plan years 5–6 _____

14. Career Development

Has the doctoral candidate prepared a professional résumé and curriculum vitae? _____

Has guidance been given on writing letters of application and on interviews?

Names of people willing to provide pastoral and academic references.

Name, title, institution

1.

2.

3.

ICETE International Council for Evangelical Theological Education
strengthening evangelical theological education through international cooperation

ICETE is a global community, sponsored by nine regional networks of theological schools, to enable international interaction and collaboration among all those engaged in strengthening and developing evangelical theological education and Christian leadership development worldwide.

The purpose of ICETE is:

1. To promote the enhancement of evangelical theological education worldwide.
2. To serve as a forum for interaction, partnership and collaboration among those involved in evangelical theological education and leadership development, for mutual assistance, stimulation and enrichment.
3. To provide networking and support services for regional associations of evangelical theological schools worldwide.
4. To facilitate among these bodies the advancement of their services to evangelical theological education within their regions.

Sponsoring associations include:

Africa: Association for Christian Theological Education in Africa (ACTEA)

Asia: Asia Theological Association (ATA)

Caribbean: Caribbean Evangelical Theological Association (CETA)

Europe: European Evangelical Accrediting Association (EEAA)

Euro-Asia: Euro-Asian Accrediting Association (E-AAA)

Latin America: Association for Evangelical Theological Education in Latin America (AETAL)

Middle East and North Africa: Middle East Association for Theological Education (MEATE)

North America: Association for Biblical Higher Education (ABHE)

South Pacific: South Pacific Association of Evangelical Colleges (SPAEC)

www.icete-edu.org

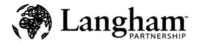

Langham Literature and its imprints are a ministry of Langham Partnership.

Langham Partnership is a global fellowship working in pursuit of the vision God entrusted to its founder John Stott –

> *to facilitate the growth of the church in maturity and Christ-likeness through raising the standards of biblical preaching and teaching.*

Our vision is to see churches in the majority world equipped for mission and growing to maturity in Christ through the ministry of pastors and leaders who believe, teach and live by the Word of God.

Our mission is to strengthen the ministry of the Word of God through:

- nurturing national movements for biblical preaching
- fostering the creation and distribution of evangelical literature
- enhancing evangelical theological education

especially in countries where churches are under-resourced.

Our ministry

Langham Preaching partners with national leaders to nurture indigenous biblical preaching movements for pastors and lay preachers all around the world. With the support of a team of trainers from many countries, a multi-level programme of seminars provides practical training, and is followed by a programme for training local facilitators. Local preachers' groups and national and regional networks ensure continuity and ongoing development, seeking to build vigorous movements committed to Bible exposition.

Langham Literature provides majority world preachers, scholars and seminary libraries with evangelical books and electronic resources through publishing and distribution, grants and discounts. The programme also fosters the creation of indigenous evangelical books in many languages, through writer's grants, strengthening local evangelical publishing houses, and investment in major regional literature projects, such as one volume Bible commentaries like *The Africa Bible Commentary* and *The South Asia Bible Commentary*.

Langham Scholars provides financial support for evangelical doctoral students from the majority world so that, when they return home, they may train pastors and other Christian leaders with sound, biblical and theological teaching. This programme equips those who equip others. Langham Scholars also works in partnership with majority world seminaries in strengthening evangelical theological education. A growing number of Langham Scholars study in high quality doctoral programmes in the majority world itself. As well as teaching the next generation of pastors, graduated Langham Scholars exercise significant influence through their writing and leadership.

To learn more about Langham Partnership and the work we do visit **langham.org**